THE PORTABLE CREEK

THE PORTABLE CREEK
— Southern Nostalgia and Other Shenanigans —

KEITH HUFFMAN

ARCHWAY PUBLISHING

Copyright © 2021 by Keith Huffman

All rights reserved. No part of this book may be used or reproduced by any means, graphic, electronic, or mechanical, including photocopying, recording, taping or by any information storage retrieval system without the written permission of the author except in the case of brief quotations embodied in critical articles and reviews.

© *Opelika-Auburn News* for columns and articles published in the *Opelika-Auburn News*. Columns and articles reprinted by permission. © *Pickens County Herald* for columns and articles published in the *Pickens County Herald*. Columns and articles reprinted by permission. © Alabama Media Group for columns published on AL.com and in *The Birmingham News*. Columns reprinted by permission. © Consolidated Publishing Co. for articles published in *The Anniston Star*. Articles reprinted by permission. Copyright, "Glory Days: Former Pro Baseball Player Reflects on Baseball Memories, Career with Giants," by *The Tuscaloosa News*, 2017. All rights reserved. Reprinted with permission.

Some of the material in this collection has been edited for content. Only minor revisions were made to keep the material as close to the original publications as possible.

Archway Publishing books may be ordered through booksellers or by contacting:

Archway Publishing
1663 Liberty Drive
Bloomington, IN 47403
www.archwaypublishing.com
844-669-3957

Because of the dynamic nature of the Internet, any web addresses or links contained in this book may have changed since publication and may no longer be valid. The views expressed in this work are solely those of the author and do not necessarily reflect the views of the publisher, and the publisher hereby disclaims any responsibility for them.

Scripture quotations are taken from the Holy Bible, New Living Translation, copyright ©1996, 2004, 2015 by Tyndale House Foundation. Used by permission of Tyndale House Publishers, a Division of Tyndale House Ministries, Carol Stream, Illinois 60188. All rights reserved.

Cover Designer: Andrew Mays
Author Photo: Kim Huffman

ISBN: 978-1-4808-9627-7 (sc)
ISBN: 978-1-4808-9626-0 (hc)
ISBN: 978-1-4808-9628-4 (e)

Library of Congress Control Number: 2020917927

Print information available on the last page.

Archway Publishing rev. date: 03/03/2021

For Kim, Kaleb, and Kason

*And to the rest of my kinfolk—
past, present, future*

CONTENTS

Foreword xi
Preface xiii

Part 1: "Wha's All the Exci'ment About?" 1

The Portable Creek 3
Paw Prints and Boyhood 8
Love Hath No Fury like a Plymouth Fury 11
Burned Luck: A Fisherman's Tragedy 16
The Bootlegger and the Shoebox 19
Football, Smack Talk, and Superstition 23
Blasphemy from a Die-Hard Football Fan:
   "Really All Just a Game" 27
Truckin' 31
Turtle Ambition and Philosophy 35
The Penny, the Matchbox, and a Fortune Worth Telling 38
Wild Cats, a Wild Man, and Bad Liquor 41
Innocently Guilty 44
Backroad Skepticism 47
The Front Porch: A True Southern Wonder 51
Love Kicks from the Sticks 54
Heartbeatings 57
Everyone Is Meaningful to Someone 61
Doe Doe of Arabia 64
Stick, Boot, and Other Proud Nicknames 67
Burning Rubber with Motorcycle Obsessions 71
Silver Bullet: A Tragic Love Story 74
P-O-T-A-T-O 78
Splinter: Every Child's Worst Nightmare 81

Love Tries ... and Some Things Are Just Meant to Last 85
I've Known Her All My Life 89
Flirting with Trouble 95
Excuses, Excuses 98
Jailhouse Shenanigans 101
Deal 'Em 105
Country Engineers 109
Joy of People 113

Part 2: Portraits: Southern Hearts, Tragedies, and Triumphs from West to East Alabama 117

Glory Days: Former Pro Baseball Player Reflects
  on Baseball Memories, Career with Giants 119
Embracing Freedom: West Alabamian's Spiritual
  Beliefs Helped Her Triumph over Addiction 129
Aliceville WWII Glider Pilot's "Longest Day" 133
All in the Break: Seizing Cues since Early Youth,
  Gordo Pool Player Reflects on Past, Love for the Game 141
A Look Back at Aubie's First Year as His Forty-
  Year Celebration Approaches 145
Sadie's Hope: Three Months after Tragedy,
  Andrews Family Embraces Hope In Mourning
  Three-Year-Old Sadie Grace 151
Park Memorial to Honor Sadie Grace Andrews 160
Answered Prayer: Sadie Grace Andrews Act Signed into Law ... 165
'A Vision to Help': Opelika Church Raises Funds
  to Buy Motorbikes for Kenya Pastors 169
Lens on the Past: How a Historic Camera Made
  Its Way from Mount Rushmore to Anniston 173
Rack 'Em Up! A Group of Old Friends Reunite over Pool 177

Part 3: "Daddy, Listen! I Think I Hear Them Growing!" 181

Sacred Coffee Creed 183
Souse Meat, Possum, and Other Exotic Delicacies 186
God Gave Us You 189
Paging Dr. Freud: A Glimpse into the Madness of Raising a Preschooler 192
Understanding the Gromis, Preschooler Model 195
Humpty Dumpty: A Quest for Healing 198
Dreamland Guests, Lingering Questions, and the Dark Rooster 201
Peculiar Visions 204
Remembering the Father-in-Law I Never Met 207
Farewell to Granny and Christmas Greetings 211
Merry Christmas, Santa 215
Enough Fun to Fill a Billfold 218
"The Avon Man" and Other Gift-Giving Exploits 221
Country Pets: Cow, Raccoon, Gator 224
Cats: They're Good People 228
Home Is Where the Birds Are 231
He's Still a Giant 234
Sympathetic Pregnancy: A Case of Mother and Son 238
Oh, Brother! 241
Watch 'Em Grow 244

Acknowledgments 249
About the Author 251

FOREWORD

When reading this book I kept thinking about a line from Broadway's *My Fair Lady*, when Professor Henry Higgins proclaims of Eliza Doolittle, "By Jove, I think she's got it."

Well, by Jove, I think this young man's got it. Not only is he a talented writer, but he understands the human condition. Be prepared to remember, laugh, smile, tear up, and maybe even cry a wee bit. Be prepared to be moved. This young man understands humanity in its many forms.

Most of these stories and essays take place in the South, in a little Alabama town called Gordo, but they have a universality that touches and unites us all.

This man's got it, and this book proves it.

Meet one of your new favorite authors.

David Housel
Athletic Director Emeritus
Auburn University
A Fellow Gordo Boy

PREFACE

This is a family memoir, of sorts, told one newspaper column at a time, a variety of memories stitched together like a patchwork quilt.

If anything, it's a heartfelt tribute to the family and folks who matter a great deal to me. Some are gone, some are still living, but I can help preserve the memories and stories they shared with me while I was growing up.

At least, this is what I've had in mind since I started contributing feature columns to newspapers and media outlets, most particularly the *Opelika-Auburn News*. I've been blessed with the opportunity to tell personal stories about myself and the people who made—and still make—meaningful marks on my life.

I grew up in the West Alabama town called Gordo, a Spanish word meaning "fat," in Pickens County. Established in 1898 and located smack-dab between Tuscaloosa and the Mississippi state line, it's home to the Gordo Green Wave and a handful of country folks who cherish everything a chicken has to offer, a good fish fry, baseball, and of course, football. Similar to Crimson Tide fans' battle cry—"Roll, Tide, Roll!"—Gordo athletic loyalists routinely chant a slightly modified version throughout football season: "Roll, Waves, Roll!"

This is my heritage, and I look back on it fondly, as do the folks who shared these memories with me. They're also to blame for inspiring me to seek out and tell other people's stories across West and East Alabama, some of which are featured in the second part of this book.

My folks certainly made growing up in a small town an extra-special experience, and I love them for it. This is my way of repaying a mighty big debt.

Keith Huffman
Opelika, Alabama

Oft, in the stilly night,
    Ere slumber's chain has bound me,
Fond memory brings the light
    Of other days around me.
—Thomas Moore,
"The Light of Other Days"

Part 1

"WHA'S ALL THE EXCI'MENT ABOUT?"

THE PORTABLE CREEK

Other than the occasional sounds of some early morning traffic, silence filled the little cemetery near the roadway. The grass was wet, the ground soft, and Pawpaw Buck Huffman led the way among the headstones.

My father, Mike "Doe Doe" Huffman, followed alongside his shuffling daddy. He'd picked the old man up to grab some breakfast at Jack's. But ol' Buck insisted they first stop by the cemetery. He had something he wanted to show off.

Approaching the spot where his daughter was buried, Buck suddenly halted and pointed down to his feet. This was it. This was where he was going to be buried—right below my father's sister, Stacy, whose grave was gifted a statue of a praying angel.

This proximity comforted ol' Buck. He cherished his sweet Monkey Doodle, whose beaming smile and blue eyes never failed to lift his spirit. Someday they'd enjoy each other's company again, in the earth and in the heavens.

But this wasn't the only thing that got Buck to grinnin'. He had another reason to be proud.

"Hey, Doe Doe!"

"Yeah, Daddy?"

Tapping a foot, Buck proclaimed, "This here's the only spot of land I ever owned."

Yessiree—Pawpaw Buck was, at long last, a happy landowner. And on June 6, 1997, he took up residence at that very spot where he'd never have to pay a cent of rent—but not before he settled the score with a very persistent country preacher, who'd set his sights on saving Buck's soul for decades.

— *Buck Wild* —

Of course, you had to be persistent to keep up with a guy like ol' stubborn Buck, whose buck-wild ways and days flirted with death on multiple occasions. His thirst for alcohol was a major contributor to this flirtation.

This was certainly the case the time he flipped his rusty car into a ditch, after hitting a curve at full speed, one night in the 1950s. At the time, a young Buck and a friend had been out joyriding through the countryside. But the joy ended when Buck and his buddy were thrown out of the car, resulting with Buck getting knocked unconscious.

When he came to, Buck gradually became aware that a white sheet was draped over him as he lay flat on his back in the grass. Sitting up slowly, his headache got an excruciating jolt from a piercing scream. It came from the woman who'd put the sheet over him, who'd mistaken him for dead. He'd never seen anyone run away so fast.

Another time, Buck decided to hop on his motorcycle and hightail it home from a Birmingham bar as a bad rainstorm absorbed the night sky. To help keep some of the rain off him, he followed closely behind an 18-wheeler—until the big truck stopped at a red light. A startled Buck somehow managed to slide under the trailer. Back then, during the late 1950s, big rigs didn't have the rear bumpers like those you see today, leaving just enough space below for something like Buck and his ride.

Heavy rain continued to pour. Buck hurried out from under the truck, banged on the window of the driver's door, and asked the confused trucker to please help pull his bike out.

He'd cheated death yet again.

Of course, there was also the time Buck got into a big argument with his daddy, Pawpaw Lee Makelin, a stout little man whose massive temper could easily rival that of any riled-up rattlesnake or red-eyed bull. Things got awfully heated awfully fast, and Buck was feeling awfully brave—and awfully drunk. If it weren't for the latter, I don't think he would have ever pulled a gun on his daddy, a decision he instantly regretted.

Because as quickly as Buck pointed the thing at him, Pawpaw Lee Make snatched it away and bashed Buck over the head with the butt. Afterward, he told his son to get up off the floor and took him to the hospital, where Buck got several stitches and time to think about the hard lesson he'd learned.

He was lucky his daddy loved him.

"We'll Bring the Creek to You"

At some point between these and other times of madness, a kind country preacher by the name of James Posey crossed paths with Buck. And almost instantly, the preacher became determined to save the ornery man's soul.

Every chance he got, Bro. Posey made a point to speak with Buck: at Buck's home, in town, in hospital rooms. In fact, the only place Buck was safe was in the bar.

Of course, Buck didn't mind the preacher, always welcoming him inside and listening as he shared the gospel. Naturally, at the end of every conversation, Bro. Posey said a prayer and never neglected to invite Buck to church.

In turn, Buck always assured the fella, who was only a few months older than him, "I'll make it out there someday." Then off to the bar Buck would go, at least until he gave up alcohol for his children.

This fact likely shocked the preacher—and literally everyone who knew Buck. This was, after all, a man who'd drink rubbing alcohol if there were no other options.

It was amazing Buck quit cold turkey. It was equally amazing that doing so didn't kill him, though it came awfully close.

Buck's family was happy to see him redeemed from addiction. But Bro. Posey still aimed to redeem Buck's soul, and his decades of pursuit, at long last, resulted with a request from Buck to be baptized. It needed to happen soon, as Buck was dying from lung cancer.

The only problem was that Buck knew he wouldn't be able to make it out to the creek.

"Don't worry about that," Bro. Posey assured him. "We'll bring the creek to you."

And so he did. The baptism took place on a sunny day under a little pavilion at the affordable housing complex where Buck lived. Sitting in his wheelchair, Buck bowed his head before a gathering of family and friends as Bro. Posey sprinkled creek water on him from a plastic cup.

Roaring applause erupted, and Bro. Posey smiled. Shortly afterward, Buck passed and was buried in the only spot of land he ever owned. But he died knowing that no matter how bad things got, the preacher and the good Lord never quit on him.

Opelika-Auburn News
SEPTEMBER 15, 2019

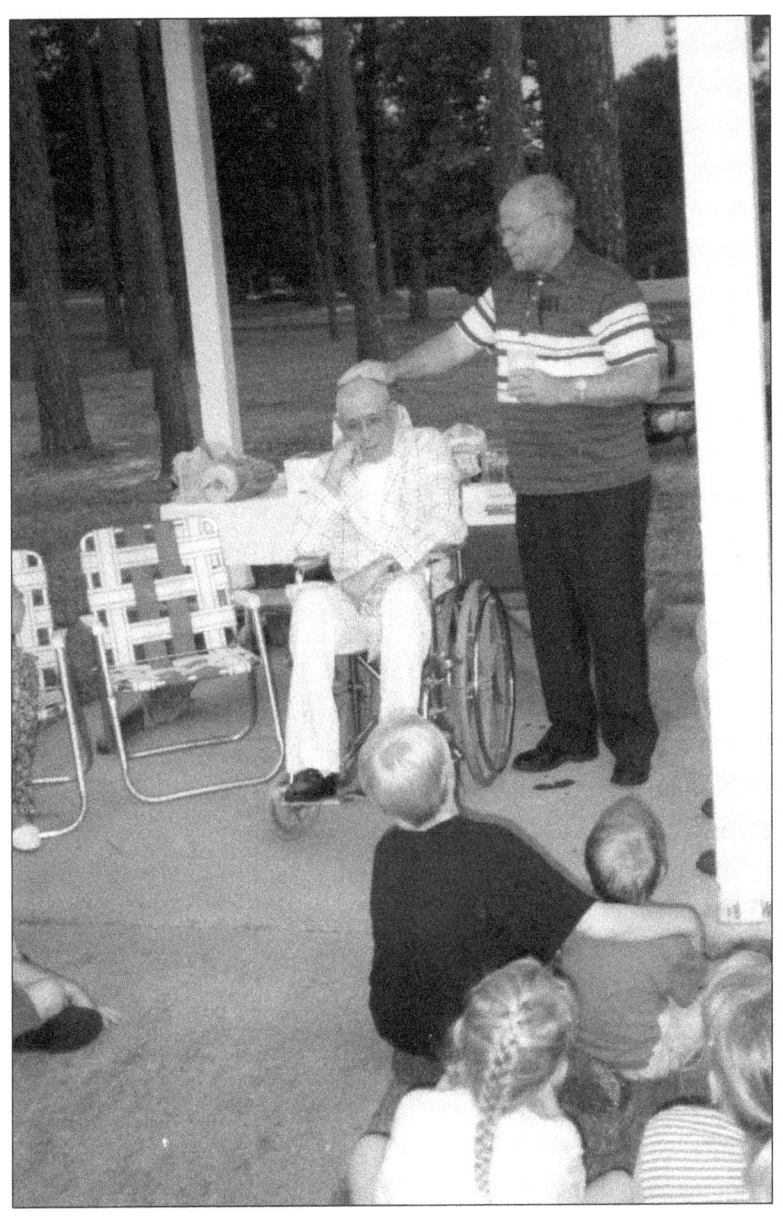

The baptism of Pawpaw Buck Huffman. My younger brother, Matt, and I are sitting across from him.

PAW PRINTS AND BOYHOOD

Stop by my desk or inside my garage, and you'll see them: dogs. Some are playing pool. Others, a high-stakes game of poker. These classic paintings by Arthur Sarnoff and Cassius Marcellus Coolidge have always held my fascination, dating back to my childhood, when I occasionally gazed into those gambling canines' eerily lifelike eyes as they stared down at me.

Often I wondered if they'd bite should they lose a game—though I knew I'd be okay if they tried. Like many young boys who grew up with tail-wagging companions, I knew my own dogs would take care of me. When it came to man's best friend, I was always dealt a great hand—like Beethoven, a German shepherd mix, whose acquaintance I gained at the pound.

A champion among great listeners, Beethoven also served as an excellent pillow as we laid carefree on the ground and interpreted Rorschach-like clouds or gazed upon stars among chirping crickets. I talked and Beethoven listened, or at least he did well pretending to listen, occasionally giving my cheek a reassuring lick.

Memories of Beethoven now surface each time I hear an exhaust fan. The day he died, I prayed and pleaded with the good Lord to bring him back. As I did so, a loud rumble suddenly rattled a nearby vent inside my grandparents' home. I was scared as I realized the Lord had heard my request among millions of other people. I immediately made repeated prayers, pleading for Beethoven to remain in heaven, instantly certain that I was ill-prepared to tend to a zombie dog. Besides, I'd read W. W. Jacobs's *The Monkey's Paw* in school and figured it was best to pay heed to the warning "Be careful what you wish for."

Stephen King's *Pet Sematary* undeniably figured into my thinking as well.

Another ace of a dog was Caleb, a black Labrador who delighted in hiding along with me and others during games of hide-and-seek. Caleb was also an ideal team member during freeze tag, given his swift agility and superb success rate in tagging those caught running in his sight. Among his favorite activities was playing on slides. He'd follow me up and down the best of them with tireless amusement.

Hooch was far less playful, but his enduring commitment to being my pal was legendary. Arriving home from school on the bus, I routinely saw Hooch waiting for me by the mailbox at the end of the driveway, his nubby tail wagging so fast it was practically invisible.

Adorable when he was a puppy, Hooch as an adult shed his cuddly features to take on a painstakingly homely appearance, complete with a largely disproportionate head attached to a jiggly body that was somehow held up by approximately three-inch legs. Still, his ugliness made him strangely attractive, a quality that only those who loved him could discern.

Frankly, it took me until around my early teen years to truly appreciate Hooch's beauty. Before then, I often preferred that he'd greet me after the school bus pulled away. That would have kept me from repeatedly having to lie to assure some riders that Hooch was the neighbor's dog each time I heard them call out, "Hey, Keith, is that your ugly dog?"

"Naw, man, I done told y'all—that's their dog over yonder!"

Good ol' Hooch—he once became lost during a short road trip and managed to find his way back to my grandparents' farm, a place he'd only been to once or twice in his life as a puppy. The farm was several miles away from where he had disappeared, but a week or so later, my pawpaw spotted my committed pooch inside the barn.

These and other furry friends throughout the years contributed unique color to my life. I miss their floppy ears, cold noses, and panting faces. And of course, their beautiful eyes, full of life and love.

Opelika-Auburn News
NOVEMBER 12, 2017

Paw prints made my boyhood special.

LOVE HATH NO FURY LIKE A PLYMOUTH FURY

Without fail, every time anger boiled within him, Uncle Floyd would stomp off his land and head up the nearest big hill, right where he knew he could be seen by those who lived on the farm across the dirt road. And it was there, atop the crest, that Uncle Floyd would hurl a variety of threats and callous words at his brother, my great-grandmother Reoma's daddy, "Poppa."

The attacks were long and loud, echoing across every acre of Poppa's farm. But the old man paid his ornery brother no mind, preferring instead to stay focused on his work in the garden or tending to animals.

Poppa's wife and children followed suit. Everyone was used to Uncle Floyd's tantrums and his blaming virtually everything he disliked on Poppa. They also were used to having one of Uncle Floyd's kids drop by later on these same evenings to ask if Poppa would go pray for their daddy. Without fail, Uncle Floyd would suddenly fall ill after his tirades and send for his brother, who'd always head on over and ask the Good Lord to please grant a healing.

The Sutton Family: Lucille, John Smelley Jr. (held by his mother in the blanket), Charlie ("Poppa"), Etta, Reoma (my great-grandmother), and Bill. Pictured in the front row are Reada and Edgar.

Poppa should have requested a longer fuse for Uncle Floyd's temper, or some holy gag order. Maybe he did. Still, in the end, love triumphed over fury.

All it took was patience—a whole lot of it.

That's something my father, Doe Doe, simultaneously did and didn't have at his disposal while consumed by personal projects when I was growing up in the 1990s. It takes phenomenal skill to rapidly switch from calm to vicious, back to serenity then venomous rage, and so on, in a single instant.

But my father not only mastered it, he perfected it. And the trophies he earned while applying this natural gift consist of the shattered hopes and dreams of "what could have been" each time he fondly reflects on projects that never reached fruition.

There is, indeed, joy in the journey, as the old saying goes. It stays true even if the journey ends in a tow truck–worthy disaster. And one of my father's most memorable journeys involved a 1970s Plymouth Fury.

— *Big Plans* —

"The Land Cruiser," we called it. That's because the heap of metal never left the spot of land in the backyard, where my father parked it after fetching it from Florida.

I remember well the first time I laid eyes on the thing, especially the instant mixed feelings of revulsion and pity that overwhelmed me as my burning eyes managed to process the sight of that tank-like monstrosity. Bearing far more rust than chipping paint the color of gray sorrow, the Land Cruiser sagged miserably and squashed the exhausted four wheels beneath it, wheels that turned into concrete blocks shortly after the car rolled up my father's driveway.

The cracked windshield offered a jagged outlook of the roadway and life in general, and the sputtering engine orchestrated one of the saddest, most despairing tunes I've ever heard. *Please, please let me rest in peace*, the car begged, refusing to crank again after my father parked it.

But Doe Doe Huffman wasn't a quitter. He had plans—big plans. He aimed to give new life to his darlin' baby and rejuvenate its clanky soul, complete with a shiny new paint job to complement shiny new wheels donning stylish spinner rims. Naturally, a bumpin' stereo system would have to be installed, plus a new tinted windshield and windows, to promote a sense of mystery and wonder of the cool daddy behind the wheel.

Indeed, my father was going to be the talk of the town, inspiring all who spotted him in his future hot rod to tap their neighbor on the shoulder and announce, "Hey, that was Doe Doe Huffman that just rode by."

Yep, big plans—but first my father had to get the Land Cruiser running again, and he was convinced he had plenty of love and patience to make it happen.

He also had lots of anger to throw in the mix—lots and lots of it. This was evidenced by the ear-splitting volume of his tantrums, plus the sheer amount of tools he hurled into the woods every time the car refused to cooperate. And yet, almost as soon as his temper boiled, it simmered and gave way to sweet talks of encouragement.

"That's okay, baby. Daddy ain't givin' up on ya."

We all wished he would, given how another wrench or screwdriver would join all the others in the woods shortly afterward. But my father was a visionary, a hopeless romantic when it came to anything bejeweled with chrome and wheels.

Mike "Doe Doe" Huffman became obsessed with driving cool vehicles at a very young age.

Admittedly, my father's determination was truly inspiring. He refused to give up, despite the passing years and his less than reassuring track record in claiming success with other projects. Love and patience, he was certain, would prevail.

And they did, in a sense, as the Land Cruiser suddenly erupted with a loud, glorious roar one day. Gripped by the realization that his unwavering devotion had finally paid off, my father rejoiced as his eyes radiated pure triumphant joy.

That is, until a joy-devouring flame shot up from under the raised hood, compelling my father to jump out of the cab and desperately use his shirt to attack the inferno that scorched his precious dream.

It was the last time the ol' Land Cruiser ever cranked. And for a while, my father sulked and fussed as the saga of the Land Cruiser became yet another memory of a possibility turned tragedy. Only this tragedy ended up as scrap metal.

In the meantime, all we could do was pray for my father's healing.

Opelika-Auburn News
JUNE 23, 2019

BURNED LUCK: A FISHERMAN'S TRAGEDY

It fed at dawn, lurking deep within the dark water, secret as a whisper confided to the departed before the casket is closed and lowered into the Earth. High above, the pinkish-blue sky inspired thoughts of cotton candy as vast ensembles of chirping crickets and croaking frogs, tuckered out from all-night performances around the pond, wound down to a mere hint of their rhythmic intensity.

The midsummer humidity, its weight made leaner from a long night's slumber, could be ignored for at least another hour. But it was always before the heat intensified when a glimpse could be caught of the giant fish as it emerged to snag some hapless prey.

As a child, I spent a lot of time at my grandparents' farm, especially during the summer when I worked around the place and helped tend to horses. Many fond memories are linked there, one of which includes the instant jackrabbit-like beat of my 11-year-old heart the first time I witnessed the great bass burst upward from the pond, located downhill from the old barn. A loud, triumphant splash followed as the magnificent creature returned to its dark dwelling, leaving behind large, wavy rings that spread toward the bank where I stood.

The bass became an instant obsession. Not only did it absolutely have to be caught, but the catcher absolutely had to be me. Images of victorious plaques filled my mind. I'd seen many displayed proudly inside bait shops and peoples' homes, the mouths of the mounted fish always gaping wide in a reenacted expression of shock that paid tribute to their fated captures.

But the gargantuan bass on my special plaque, no doubt, would rival all of these, reducing them to mere minnows. Naturally, local fame and a huge write-up in the newspaper would follow, subsequently prompting an eager editor from *Field & Stream* to reach out and produce an in-depth piece worthy of a hat tip from Hemingway.

The smell of fish magnified the madness that engulfed me. Shortly after first spotting my prey, I nonchalantly approached Pawpaw Jim Sanders and sparked up some small talk about the best ways to catch a gigantic bass that just possibly—just *theoretically* now —could be caught in his very pond.

I tried all of his suggestions, using a variety of rods. I baited ornery crickets, wriggling worms, and lures of various colors, shapes, and sizes. From daylight to dusk, I fished, in shallow and deep water. Many days passed miserably, as I managed to snag numerous bream, plus a catfish or two. But the great bass, alas, remained elusive. Often my grandparents joined me, and I'd eye them suspiciously—alarmingly—anytime a remote hint of a catch occurred. My heart sank with their bobbers.

This craziness lasted forever. Weeks turned into months, and the soul-draining failures tallied up heavily against my unfulfilled obsession. Spirit drooping, I eventually figured it best to preoccupy my mind with other things, to avoid losing whatever remained of my sanity.

That's when my bobber sank. Initially bearing not a trace of faint hope for catching anything worthwhile, I ecstatically lifted and pulled my cane pole with all my might. Something mighty heavy pulled the other way.

Embroidered wisdom on an old flour sack hanging reverently in my garage states, "All the planning in the world can't beat dumb luck." I believe that now, and I started believing it then. I also believe few devout Christians have ever prayed as hard as I did during my intense tug-of-war.

My promises to the Almighty grew in extravagance the closer I got the great fish to the bank, and I yelped with glee as the gilled monster hung triumphantly before my face. Suddenly, though, it dropped free to the ground with a loud "thwump," instantly flopping about in a desperate attempt to reach the water.

Fueled with world-defying adrenaline, I did what any self-respecting fisherman would have done: I belly flopped on top of it, practically face-planting in the dirt as I wrestled with the gasping creature, its bulging eyes glaring defiantly as it dished out a fight-and-flight combo. An epic struggle ensued, but it was I who prevailed and hauled my prize to my grandparents' home.

Eager to weigh my catch (I was certain that joker was a hundred pounds or more), I hurried over to Pawpaw Jim, who promised he'd take me to the bait shop as soon as he could. We'd also see how much it would cost to mount the thing. Until then, I could keep the great fish in his freezer—an offer I declined. My grandparents love to fry fish, so I determined it wise to preserve my special catch in the freezer in the backyard shed of my own house. Besides, I knew I'd occasionally want to admire my stunning capture.

I should've listened to the old man. Before we were able to make that bait shop trip to document history, as I was away at school daydreaming about the prize-winning plaque that would hang gloriously in my bedroom, our shed caught fire. Nothing was salvaged—nothing, except the memory of my great loss. There were plenty more fish in the sea—or pond—I was assured. Still, my fisherman's heart longs for the bass that got away.

Opelika-Auburn News
SEPTEMBER 30, 2018

THE BOOTLEGGER AND THE SHOEBOX

A big surprise—that's what Henry Sanders, my great-grandfather, was going to give his wife and family.

It was the early 1950s, and my grandfather was getting ready to go to Korea, where he and other U.S. soldiers would be instructed, right as they were stepping off a transporting aircraft, to zigzag while dashing to a specified area in case of enemy fire. Korea, likewise, would be the place where my grandfather would try his first—and last—bowl of cornflakes with beer during a period of critically low supplies.

Furthermore, Korea would also be where an enemy soldier would sneak into camp one night and slash the wall of the tent where my grandfather slept, putting a permanent scar right above his foot. Prior to this sneak attack, my grandfather would change sides on his cot because of the unlevel ground, laying his head down where his feet originally had been. If he hadn't, it likely would have been his throat that got cut.

But, on this particular night before his experiences in the Korean War, my grandfather was going to surprise everyone by showing up earlier than expected for a visit from Fort Benning, Georgia.

Henry Sanders (right) stands with a fellow soldier.

Having ridden buses and hitchhiked his way to his hometown of Gordo, Alabama, my grandfather was on foot as he walked along country roads toward the Kennie Hill community. He was wishing someone could give him a lift, when a pair of headlights suddenly flashed from behind. By the time he threw up a thumb, an old car nearly left him in its dust.

It came to a gravel-flinging halt, its back tires abruptly rising and slamming back down. A deep voice called out, and my grandfather rushed over.

"Where ya headin'?" the driver asked, his tone indicating there was zilch time to dawdle.

My grandfather told him.

"Hop in."

The ride was pure insanity, death-defying, as the car careened wildly around every curve and catapulted many feet after every hill. My grandfather desperately seized anything he could hold on to, his thoughts solely focused on praying for his dear life. Unfazed, the driver never eased off the gas, delivering my grandfather to his destination in record time—unbroken, the same as all the clinking jars of moonshine in the back seat. My grandfather considered asking the driver for one. He reckoned he'd earned it.

— *Shoebox Surprise* —

This certainly wasn't the first time my kinfolks got caught up in bootlegging shenanigans. There was the time my grandfather's daddy, Alf, got a shoebox surprise. This happened during the early 1930s, when prohibitionists were hell-bent on eliminating every last drop of alcohol, resulting in the underground economic boom of whiskey, moonshine, and rum-distributing entrepreneurs.

One of these country business folks was a young fella by the name of John Falls, who'd taken quite a fancy to Alf's oldest daughter, Lorene. Aiming to butter up her daddy and ask for Lorene's hand in marriage, John made his way to Alf's home, toting a shoebox containing a pint of whiskey under his arm. Upon arriving, he set the gift on a table, where it would be waiting for Alf when he got home.

The wait wasn't too long, as a hot-tempered Alf walked through the front door and carried on an argument he was having with the man behind him: the sheriff.

"I don't care what you say," the sheriff said. "I know you're hidin' alcohol in here somewhere."

"No, I ain't!" Alf said. "There ain't no alcohol in this house. I'll even help you look."

So he did, accompanying the sheriff as every cabinet, cupboard, room, and closet was thoroughly searched—all to no avail.

Finally, the sheriff spotted the shoebox. "What's in the box?"

Alf sneered, boldly declaring, "Ain't nothin' in that there box! Here, I'll show ya."

I'm willing to bet good money that Alf was far more surprised than anyone else in the house.

And so Alf and John, who'd returned to the house with Lorene around the time of the big shoebox reveal and fessed up that he was the one who brought the whiskey, were taken to jail. Shortly afterward, however, a deal was struck. Long before the shoebox fiasco, the sheriff had approached Alf on many occasions, requesting he paint the town of Gordo's water tower—for free, out of the kindness of his heart. Alf, naturally, told the sheriff where he could kindly shove it. Now, the deal was Alf and John would both paint the water tower. It was community service, you see. In turn, the whole whiskey matter would be dropped.

The next morning, Alf and John were dropped off at the tower, along with paint and brushes. The sheriff would later return to retrieve them, and this routine would go on until the job was finished. In the meantime, if anyone flaked out, the sheriff knew where they lived.

Ready to get the whole thing over, Alf climbed to the top and got to work. John, meanwhile, stayed on the ground. He was afraid of heights.

"Might as well come on up here!" Alf called down to him. "We gotta start painting from the top. Ain't a thing you can do down there!"

It was about this time that a freight train whistle could be heard approaching on some nearby tracks.

"The hell there ain't!" John replied, and he soon hopped aboard a passing boxcar, waving goodbye to his future father-in-law.

Poor Alf—he'd gotten yet another big surprise.

Opelika-Auburn News
JANUARY 5, 2020

FOOTBALL, SMACK TALK, AND SUPERSTITION

Aunt Lorene, my great-grandfather's sister, used to assure folks that if she told you something three times, it's gotta be true—guaranteed. But I don't reckon I'll have to tell anyone thrice that yet another glorious football season has kicked off, bringing with it all the wonderful things that unite and divide us.

Rich traditions. Intense rivalries. Color-coded allegiances. Beloved and despised coaches, players and sports commentators. Bonfires, tailgating, and other game-day gatherings. Spirit-bolstering cheers. And smack talk—lots and lots of venomous, teeth-gnashing, egomaniacal smack talk.

For many, this compulsive jabbering serves as the hub, the essence or driving force, of the season. Virtually no one is safe from the skunk-eyed sneers and brutal vocabularies that spew out of the loud mouths of strangers, so-called friends, and family. Blood may, indeed, be thicker than water; but wearing a shirt with a dye deemed the wrong color could cause an admirable family man or woman to get dog-cussed and condemned by an otherwise doting grandparent.

"That fool oughta know better'n be seen wearin' that god-awful trash! Some folks just have no class and good for nothin'. Plum embarrasin'!"

— *Laying the Smack Down* —

Yessiree, football fanatics are an ultrasensitive breed, and this sensitivity cuts even deeper among folks like my Roll Tide father and our War Eagle cousin, Barry. Bloodthirsty, the two lock horns after every Iron Bowl, in fierce, ritualistic fashion, typically through a heated phone call initiated by the one aiming to gloat as soon as the game's over.

"How 'bout them Tigers?"

"Man, you ain't called me all year, and now you got the gall to come at me 'bout some lame Tigers."

The smack-talk battlefield gets awful bloody from there, with the two men practically lunging at each other's throat as they pass ego-scarring blows with every seething remark. At some point, depending on how bad the losing team got their fannies handed to them, a ceasefire is called. But these truces are always very short-lived. The war rages on.

Still, I reckon Barry's lucky he's family. Otherwise, he may get the kind of no-holds-barred verbal brawl my father once had during a high school football game with someone's equally quick-tempered granny, who certainly held her own during the clash. At the time, my father wasn't too impressed with a young quarterback, and his loudly voicing his blunt opinion instantly jolted the granny into fist-shaking defense mode. Nobody was gonna talk bad about her grandbaby—nobody.

Their smack-talk showdown was epic, and certainly far more thrilling than anything that was happening on the field at the time. But when the fuse is lit, smack talkers are gonna do what they do best.

Just ask my pal, Doug, another Tide fan who's always at odds with his younger brother, the orange-and-blue Roddy, who's prone to wearing jerseys of the teams opposing Bama on game days. The two compete in everything: card games, board games, and especially croquet.

In fact, it was during a heated croquet match that a fuming Doug gave voice to a phenomenally profound statement, one that belongs on a banner or monument. If anything, it'll be engraved on Doug's tombstone: "If you'll cheat in croquet, you'll cheat in life."

Wise words to live by, folks.

But when they're not dueling with mallets, these brothers are feuding over SEC football. And this, naturally, bleeds into other things, like birthday gifts for their Bama-crazed mama.

"Hey, Mom, how 'bout I get you a flag with all of Bama's national championships on it?" Doug once said.

Oh yeah, she'd like that.

"And I could get you something with Auburn's championships too, Mom," a grinning Roddy chimed in.

Doug couldn't help it. He saw an opening and went in for the smackdown: "Yeah, you could get it put on a little napkin. That should be big enough."

— *Superstitious Banning* —

Nope, it simply wouldn't be football season without some good ol' smack talk—or superstition. You can't be too careful when it comes to doing your part to help assure your team's triumph. So you can't blame a guy or gal for routinely wearing their lucky, raggedy game-day shirt that's been passed down for generations and can barely cut it as a suitable washrag.

You'd also be wise to hold your tongue when another fan clings to a lucky rabbit's foot, or when they cradle a sacred snow globe containing a miniature figure of their team's mascot, or clutch a crucifix or commemorative Paul "Bear" Bryant Coca-Cola bottle, while pleading to God to please, please let the game go right.

It's this exact kind of thinking that got me and my wife permanently banned from a friend's home on a certain day of the year: the Iron Bowl. This decision was made shortly after the last time we watched a game at our friend's home. That day was November 30, 2013, when the mind-blowing "Kick Six" made history at Jordan-Hare Stadium.

Before that final play, there'd been plenty of smack talk hurled at the TV. But our friend suddenly became speechless, eerily quiet, after witnessing Auburn's Chris Davis catch the Tide's 57-yard field goal attempt and then dash 100 yards to win the game, 34–28.

As a future precaution, my wife and I were told we wouldn't be welcomed back to watch another Iron Bowl, simply because our being there that day must have somehow, in some way, interfered with the Tide's destiny.

We understood. It was too risky. No need to tell us thrice.

Opelika-Auburn News
SEPTEMBER 1, 2019

BLASPHEMY FROM A DIE-HARD FOOTBALL FAN: "REALLY ALL JUST A GAME"

Thousands of fans cheered wildly, dauntingly, from the mounted TV in my garage as I trailed the old man in shooting pool. Finally, he missed and turned his attention to the SEC game. Stooping forward to try and knock a solid into a corner pocket, I was just about to fire the cue ball when the remark came: "But you know, at the end of the day, it's really all just a game."

Overwhelming shock seized the moment, halting time and giving my junk food–packed gut an unnervingly hollow sensation. My feet felt numb, and my eyes stared unblinkingly, gravely, at the old man who stood before me. I knew exactly what I'd heard, but I wanted to be absolutely certain that he was referring to the thing he loved dearly, rather than our little billiards competition.

"Beg pardon?"

"It's really all just a game," he said. "Football."

Totally unprepared for this moment, I tightened my grip on my cue. It was my only defense against any type of catastrophic mayhem—physical, mental or spiritual—that such a perplexing moment could likely unleash. We'd been talking about the Crimson Tide, who the old man routinely deemed as the most divine of all SEC teams, when he, my father Mike "Doe Doe" Huffman, allowed his conscious mind to make those words audible: "really all just a game."

I questioned if there was a hotline I should call, some emergency outlet available for those who witness firsthand such treasonous remarks uttered by the very ones others regard as official measuring sticks for gaging and comparing magnitudes of college football fandom. Could I be charged as an accomplice for not reporting the incident? How would other family and friends take the news? Would they understand? *Could* they understand?

I continued to stare at my father as he stood across the table, oblivious to the sheer significance of his statement. My gaze was suddenly drawn to his crimson shirt. Naturally, it was the color he'd worn all those times I'd watched him launch into celebratory dances while shouting praise each time the Tide scored a touchdown. The intensity of his dancing reached whole new levels when Alabama claimed victory, the quality of his movements somehow alternating between swanlike grace and the wounded waddle of an expiring duck.

"It feels like seeing your firstborn child for the first time," he remarked when Bama claimed its 2011 national title.

Through wishful telepathy, my father often talked coaches, players, and referees through plays and penalties. When first downs, scores, and "good calls" were made, he commended their respective wit, sharp eyes, agility, and integrity. Otherwise, he typically jolted from his chair, cold eyes glaring, and furiously stomped about the room, while unleashing heated assortments of vicious obscenities toward the TV. I truly sympathize with the poor angel who has to recite those vulgarities when my father faces the Good Lord on Judgment Day.

During times when mere seconds ticked harshly away as the Tide needed a single touchdown to clench victory, my father fretfully paced about, the tension and his anxiety overwhelming the room several times greater than the thickest humidity on a boiling summer day. Genuine fear in his blue eyes, he often reached for his phone to call or text a relative, seeking any assurance that a happy ending would prevail.

"Don't worry, hun," a relative would tell him. "I've got Coach on speed dial. It's all gonna be alright."

Watching games with my father required a strong tolerance for extreme energy—positive and negative. Win or lose, his deeply impassioned reactions often drove others out of his home.

Of course, his reactions didn't stop when the game was over. Throughout weeks following Saturday victories, my father pranced about like a jubilant child heading to a bounty of presents under a Christmas tree, his faith in humanity renewed. His demeanor changed considerably, however, when the Tide lost: his steps became heavier from shackles of depression, and his sour mood reflected his disappointment. The world was a rotten, cold, and cruel place, especially for those bearing crimson souls, what with all the cheating committed by other teams and those god-awful calls by refs conspiring against the Tide.

My father's obsession engulfed him, making him ultrasensitive to any sports criticism or notion of another family member somehow managing to get a closer view of the Tide on game days. Once, during the time my wife and I were dating, we received press passes to watch Bama play from the press box at Bryant-Denny Stadium. Fully aware that I was about to poke a bear already well-set in battle mode, I texted a picture of Kim and I sitting together as thousands of fans roared in the distance behind us. My father's reactions ranged from shock to sheer frustration because I didn't take him instead, to genuine sorrow that he had somehow raised such a heartless son with the audacity to torment him in such a way.

After my wife and I moved to Opelika, my father assured me that if his grandson, Kaleb, wore an Auburn outfit during visits home to Gordo, our impressionable toddler would promptly return to Opelika wearing Alabama memorabilia. I'd expect nothing less from the man who years ago made it well-known how he wanted to be buried in a crimson casket and suit at his funeral, Lynyrd Skynyrd's "Free Bird" setting the tone while being lowered into the ground.

"Really all just a game." My father later elaborated on this remark, citing health concerns. "Don't get me wrong, I love my Tide," he said. "But I'm not about to work myself into a heart attack. Gettin' old. Gotta be careful, you know."

I reckon some truth rang clear in his words. There are more important things than football, like not losing too many games of pool to a hustling father.

Opelika-Auburn News
NOVEMBER 19, 2017

The Crimson Hustler

TRUCKIN'

Quiet now. Don't make a peep. Just stay in the back, and don't move.

Those were my instructions, and you better believe I muted and paused, my ears tuned in to every word uttered in the exchange that followed. I was lying on the bunk in the back of the 18-wheeler's cab, hidden under a thin blanket and pillow. My hideout was perfect—total camouflage. In fact, the only thing that could possibly give me away was the obvious figure of a kid lying flat on his back, toes pointing upward, under a blanket, the subtle motion of the pillow atop my head paralleling my every breath.

My father, Doe Doe, was at the wheel, talking to someone at a weigh station, verifying his log book, fuel permit, and insurance. Neither his job nor his insurance allowed for any unauthorized people—especially hitchhiking young'uns—to ride along. And yet, after an eternity spent hinting, prompting, and begging, there I was, ready to hit the highway for a week inside an 80,000-pound mass of rolling steel.

Our ultimate destination was a warehouse in Laredo, Texas, but we had to make stops in Mississippi and Louisiana as well. My father mapped out our entire voyage the weekend prior, studying his trusty road atlas and jotting down many notes for his route, all to make sure everything went smooth-ish.

As for my duties, I had to stay out of sight when we came upon any weigh stations. Of course, the perpetual sneeze-inducing tickle in my nose wasn't helping, nor was the massive mosquito bite on my leg that kept demanding some scratchin'. The odds seemed stacked against me, and there was certainly no better feeling than the rush of relief that hit when the truck started rolling again.

"All right. You good. You can come back out now."

Yessiree. The open road: plenty of miles to cover, sights to see, bull to talk—and please don't forget those opportunities to blow the horn at any gesturing travelers.

Naturally, the radio was tuned to rock stations, giving voice to Lynyrd Skynyrd, AC/DC, and the Rolling Stones. They and many others sang us from truck stop to truck stop, where we'd stop for a bite to eat after leaving many miles in our dust. Greasy BBQ plates and bottles of Mountain Dew were always in high demand at these joints, a fact that significantly contributed to a doctor telling my father years later that he wouldn't be surprised at all if ol' Doe Doe keeled over before reaching the office door to leave. Bad cholesterol will do that to you.

But it would be many years before thoughts of healthy dieting would surface and haunt my mind. Instead, I devoted most of my attention to the other folks occupying the truck stops and rest areas, wondering if I'd encounter any like the ones I'd heard about from my father and his fellow truckers. There was the time my father's buddy, Frank, stopped to use the restroom in a sketchy part of New York City, only to have the stall suddenly swing open and a gun stuck in his face. "Gimme ya wallet."

Frank complied. He was in no position to protest.

While never robbed, my father was definitely no stranger to hustlers, cons and deadbeats.

Once, while trucking through Virginia during Christmastime, he was approached by a man who said he was trying to buy a bus ticket home. Agreeing to help the fella, my father reached for his wallet and pulled out two bucks. But this was highly upsetting to the ticketless man, who saw there was more cash in that wallet. The guy proceeded to cuss my father, his breath reeking of cheap spirits. Two dollars won't buy you no stinkin' bus ticket home to catch Santa.

Won't buy you a bottle of wine, either.

But I learned that folks will go without a lot of things. My father proved this by offering to buy food or gas for those folks who moseyed on up and made the case about how they desperately needed some money for these things. Only, instead of taking him up on his offers, they'd usually drop the matter and split, grumbling about the unfairness of it all.

Now, don't get me wrong. We met some charming folks too—wisecrackin' waitresses; mysterious gals who knocked on truck doors late at night to check and see if anyone was feeling a smidge too lonesome; and of course, truckers—bookoos of miles-devouring truckers. One of the biggest gatherings of them was at a truck stop in Texas, where truckers of all shapes, shades, and sizes exchanged road stories and dirty jokes, sharing their unique accents.

I sat in a corner of the dining area, reading a book I'd brought for the trip. Rather, I pretended to read. I was far more interested in what those grown folks were saying, a lot of which I wouldn't fully understand until I got a lot older. Suddenly, a waitress appeared, hands on her hips and face scowling, raising her voice to dominate over all the others: "Hey! It's too loud over there! And stop all that cussin'!"

Abruptly, my father turned to me: "Boy, what're you cussin' out loud over there for?"

"I'm not talkin' to him," the waitress scolded. "He ain't made a peep. I'm talkin' about y'all."

Yeah. Stop all that cussin'. Now go wash your mouths out with soap.

I teased my father about this until the matter got so old, it went senile. But ol' Doe Doe got me back. As we started driving back from Laredo, a city on the Mexican border, it was time once again for me to hide in the back of the cab. Seeming to put a lot more weighted emphasis on his words, my father repeated his warning that he could seriously lose his job if I were spotted, and I'd be hauled off to who-knows-where in the process.

So back under the blanket and pillow I went, ears alert.

"Anybody traveling with you?"

"Just my son."

That traitor! I jolted upward but remained on the bunk, at least until the truck started rolling again. I heard my father: "All right. You good. You can come back out now."

He was laughing as I re-emerged, telling me we didn't stop at another weigh station. That time it was the border patrol.

Opelika-Auburn News
MARCH 15, 2020

TURTLE AMBITION AND PHILOSOPHY

She wanted to be a princess when she grew up. That was my friend's dream when she was little. And she was certain that if she really believed with all her heart, then her dream would come true.

But she encountered a serious doubter, a nonbeliever in the notion that a fellow Alabamian could ascend to a royal throne. My friend was told she couldn't be a princess when she grew up. She could be a lot of things, but becoming a princess was out of the question.

It was impossible.

This realization, uncompromising with its sharp sting, was hard to accept—especially after many of us were repeatedly assured, at church and elementary school, that nothing was impossible. All you had to do was believe in yourself.

My friend, alas, must have lost the faith—at least to an extent. She remains a castle-less peasant like the rest of us, with no enchanted kingdom to invest in real estate. But she did meet her Prince Charming, a noble guy from Tennessee who treats her like a princess, somewhat.

Still, I truly sympathize with her. I understand exactly how it feels to have your childhood dream, your life-defining passion, ripped away by boring reality.

I wanted to be a turtle. And for a while, I was able to defy reality, using empty boxes for my shell. Making holes in the sides for my bony bird legs, I walked around bowlegged and slow, as is custom among shell-dwelling reptiles.

Naturally, my speed got a phenomenal boost when I mutated into a nunchaku- or sword-wielding ninja turtle. After all, swift speed and radical weaponry are utmost necessities when you routinely have to save the world from utter chaos.

Being a ninja turtle had its perks, especially the meal plan. This special type of turtle devours pizza, while all the regular turtles typically feast on vegetables, fruits, bugs, and dog food. Take my word: cheesy pizza with virtually any topping is far more appetizing than dry dog kibble.

Still, ninja or simply ordinary, I just wanted to be a turtle—period. That's why I devoted so much time to studying them, begging my parents and grandparents to pull over on the side of the road the moment I spotted one. Besides checking out library books about my favorite reptiles, I also made a point to join my grandparents when they fished. They could keep all the bass, bream, and catfish. My eyes were on the red-eared sliders and snapping turtles that stole their bait.

Observing all those turtles taught me a great deal about their watchful and steady approaches to life. Plus, I was fascinated by the fact that they could pull back inside their shells anytime they wanted, content in their own private little worlds. There also was a distinct calmness about them, one which later impressed upon me a sense of wisdom that most things will be okay, as long as you stay level-headed, patient, and prepared to use whatever personal strengths the Good Lord gave you.

Insight from Turtle Philosophy 101 may sound cliché, but I often wish I'd shown more level-headedness and patience when life doled out some challenges, especially the times when I stubbornly bit off more trouble than I could chew. Snapping turtles apparently didn't get the memo, either. Readily lashing out at the slightest hint of any nuisance, they undeniably could use some serious anger management classes. Of course, their heads are too big to completely retract into their spiky shells, so I reckon they had to toughen up.

If life hands you lemons, devour them.

My childhood dream of someday becoming a turtle stayed with me for a while during my early elementary school days, at least until I wore my first turtleneck sweater. I still can't stand shirts with tight collars agitating my neck, although I've learned over the years to tolerate wearing ties on special occasions.

But turtlenecks ruined the whole thing for me. I also realized my back wasn't hardening into a shell, and I didn't have a good supply of boxes to keep pretending I had one. I'd lost the faith.

Eventually, I decided to pursue another dream. And yet, sometimes I still wonder how life as a turtle would have turned out.

Opelika-Auburn News
JANUARY 6, 2019

THE PENNY, THE MATCHBOX, AND A FORTUNE WORTH TELLING

A witch once cured me of a wart that staked its claim on my left thumb. At least, the mysterious, middle-aged lady assured an approximately 10-year-old me that she was a witch. And all she needed for her spell to work was a penny and an empty matchbox.

Clenching the coin in a manner paralleling the steady grip of a seasoned surgeon holding a scalpel, the witch took my hand and rubbed the wart with both sides of the one-cent magic ingredient. Securing the coin inside the matchbox, she then gave me simple—though vital—instructions: "Now, as soon as you get home, go on and take the matchbox into the woods and hide it in a spot where no one will ever find it. After you do that, forget all about the penny and the matchbox."

My parents would have phoned the local meteorologist to verify hell's blizzard if they'd seen how well I followed those directions. Days passed, maybe weeks—these details are fuzzy. What remains crystal clear is the wart's absence—a realization that left me flabbergasted when I last reached to pick at the seed-bearing devil and discovered it was gone, mysteriously banished from my hand without a trace.

Years later, during my psychology studies, I learned about a phenomenon called the "placebo effect," in which peoples' genuine beliefs in given treatments has reportedly resulted with medical improvements, despite their having been given sugar or water pills. Of course, the participants were unaware of the sheer bogusness of the "treatments" they received. Perhaps there's a link between the placebo effect and my wart's disappearance. Of course, die-hard skeptics may just as reasonably blame the supernatural. Very likely, we'll never know.

One thing for certain, however, is my family has had its fair share of encounters with magical well-wishers, like my great-grandfather, who grew up in the West Alabama town of Gordo during the Depression. Once, when he was a child, a caravan of carnival folk visited the town, and an old lady who claimed to be psychic called out to him. She wanted to tell him his fortune.

"Look, lady, I don't have any money I can give you," he told her.

"I know. You ain't got nothin' but a penny in your pocket," she said before proceeding to share her vision, free of charge:

"One day you're gonna go overseas and find a gold mine."

My grandfather thanked her and went on with his life. Now fast-forward to the 1950s and the Korean War. Serving in the U.S. Army Air Forces, my grandfather was among other soldiers who survived frigid winter conditions while advancing toward the Yalu River that divides North Korea and China.

Late one afternoon during his time in Korea, my grandfather and a comrade ventured into a village they'd been instructed to stay away from, their curiosities too strong to halt. A tiny shop displayed ink pens in a window, and the two soldiers stepped inside to see what else was for sale.

Apparently, though, the shop was supposed to have been closed. A great panic erupted as two Korean men and the two soldiers locked eyes. Between them sat a scale on a table toward the back of the store. And by the scale was a bucket of gold dust the Korean men had been weighing.

Behind the Korean men, a drawn curtain occasionally moved. Convinced someone was quietly waiting behind the curtain, my grandfather gestured to the pens in the window and did his best to assure the shopkeepers that all he wanted was to buy one.

He rushed out after making the purchase, and my grandfather and his friend hurried back to their fellow soldiers. During their trek back, his friend asked if they should tell someone about what they'd seen.

Thinking it over, my grandfather said, "Nah. Besides, it wouldn't be us who got to keep anything."

This comment likely jogged his memory of the old fortune-teller's vision years prior. She hadn't fibbed. "The old lady told me I'd find a gold mine," my grandfather once told me. "But she never said I'd get to keep it."

Opelika-Auburn News
OCTOBER 28, 2018

WILD CATS, A WILD MAN, AND BAD LIQUOR

Paul "Bear" Bryant won his enduring nickname in his teens by wrestling a muzzled carnival bear, or so the legend goes. He was supposed to have won a dollar for every minute he spent in the ring, but the bear's owner flaked out on the deal.

Alf Sanders, my maternal great-great grandfather, once fought a caged bobcat that had been caught in the Sipsey swamp in Pickens County. His prize was $50 and a brand-new suit of clothes. And he collected his winnings—sho'nuff.

The showdown happened during the early twentieth century, and it's chronicled in a front-page article in the July 18, 1935, issue of the *Pickens County Herald and West Alabamian*. Written 30 years after the whole thing went down, the article bears a captivating title: "Bad Liquor and Wild Cats: A True Story from Pickens."

According to the article and my great-grandfather, Henry Sanders, who told me this story about his dad on multiple occasions, a wire cage containing the wild cat was brought into downtown Gordo, where it was parked in front of a local saloon. The setup attracted a large gathering of folks, who read the message on a placard that hung above the cage: "$25.00 reward to the owner of any dog that ... whips ... this wild cat."

The *Herald* article stated, "The cat was an extra-large one, with the strength of a lion. He was in no humor for foolishness. His great white teeth showing between his snarling lips and his curling gray claws like briar hooks, extending from his heavy

41

set feet, were warnings to any man or beast who might come in contact with him." The challenge and hefty reward, the article said, soon attracted a competitor, who emerged from the crowd and brought forth his large, undefeated bulldog, Bulger. However, the wild cat wasted no time proving that he was in a far tougher league.

Collecting $25 from Bulger's distraught owner, the cat's owner welcomed any new takers. The wait wasn't long, as my grandfather Alf made his way toward the crowd. Described by the *Herald* as a "red-faced, slender young man weighing about 150 pounds," Alf addressed those gathered, voicing his curiosity: "Wha's all the exci'ment about?"

The proposition was explained to him, and Alf—who'd taken quite a few snorts of hard liquor that day—peered into the cage and saw not one cat ... but two. Asking which one was being bet on, Alf was told there was only one cat. Peering again into the cage, he dismissed the remark.

"You cain't fool me," Alf was quoted in the *Herald*. "I know two cats from one, but I'll tell you what I'll do. I'll whip both of them cats bare handed for twenty-five dollars. I can lick any damn wild cat in Alabama."

This got the crowd excited, and $25 was quickly raised for Alf's entry. If he won, Alf would get the entry fee, plus $25 from the cat's owner.

Giving the signal—"Open the door"—Alf entered the cage. Locking eyes on the cats, he dove after them, but they swiftly dodged.

"I knowed all the time you was a damn coward," Alf roared at the cats, per his quote in the *Herald*. "I can lick all the wild cats in Sipsey swamp at one time."

The fight was on. Teeth gnashed, bodies clashed, claws slashed. Unleashing a fierce scream, the vicious cat ripped Alf's shirt completely off, causing the flabbergasted wild man to call out and alert the crowd that his shirt was gone.

"Keep goin'," the crowd cheered. They'd get him a new shirt.

The spectacle continued, and the cat next laid waste to Alf's pants. Again, he alerted the crowd.

"Keep goin'," they cheered. They'd get him some new pants.

Alf kept goin'. In fact, he managed to keep goin' so well that the cat's owner started hollerin' at Alf to stop: "You're gonna kill my cat!"

"Well, by God," Alf was quoted in the *Herald*, "count him out then, and open the door."

The owner did just that. Heaving the dog-tired cat aside, an equally exhausted Alf rushed out of the cage, victorious.

The crowd praised the local victor, who was covered in blood and sported what little remained of his clothes: his shoes.

It was in this pitiful shape that a very sober Alf gladly accepted his $50 prize—and as promised, a brand-new suit of clothes.

For all this, Alf owed thanks to the bad liquor that fueled his courage ... or his madness.

Opelika-Auburn News
AUGUST 4, 2019

INNOCENTLY GUILTY

Everybody in my early elementary school class gathered 'round. We knew the drill. Circle Time had arrived, and we were all antsy to listen once again to the special speaker, who always greeted us from his soapbox that was our teacher's knee: McGruff the Crime Dog.

Donning a snazzy beige trench coat, plaid pants, and leather dress shoes, McGruff routinely summoned our teacher to help him down from his lookout spot by the window. He'd talk with us about a variety of things aimed to reduce crime and the number of intakes at drug rehab centers across the globe. All we had to do was listen closely and heed McGruff's candid advice, and we'd be helping him "take a bite out of crime!" Or if anything, get a good nibble.

Following McGruff's final remarks, our teacher always emphasized the highlights to help drive home our pal's message: "That's right, y'all. Tax fraud is a very serious crime that the IRS doesn't take to kindly. So don't pull any fast ones, and always remember to embrace honesty when filing your future taxes."

Okay, so maybe McGruff's messages weren't quite that deep. But you get the gist.

I liked McGruff and really didn't mind doing what I could to make his job easier. That is, until a couple of his talks really hit home—hard.

The whole mess happened shortly after everyone plopped down one day for Circle Time. It had seemed like any other elementary school day. I'd finished my fair share of coloring and counting, feigned renewed interest in a Dr. Seuss book I'd flipped through dozens of times, and recited my alphabet as a classmate raised a wooden yardstick to tap each letter posted high on the wall. There was no time for idle minds in my kindergarten class.

Finally, it was time to lend our ears to our favorite crime-fighting canine.

"Hello, kids."

"Hi, McGruff!"

Instinctively, ol' McGruff launched into another one of his antidrug sermons, fixing those perpetually stern eyes on each of us. At first it seemed we were just getting yet another crucial reminder to refuse any offers from shifty-eyed dope dealers lurking in the shadows, all of them just itching to trap us in some serious addictions and gain a steady influx of our milk money. But McGruff threw us a curveball, one that pinpointed a specific addictive danger in our midst: nicotine.

"Say 'no' to cigarettes," McGruff told us. "They make breathing hard and put our lives in danger."

A stickler to routine, our teacher again underscored McGruff's imparted wisdom: "That's right. Don't smoke cigarettes, y'all."

The message was straightforward, but it really didn't sink in until my next visit with my grandparents that same week.

Flicking his lighter, Pawpaw Jim lit an L&M tucked between his lips and took a long drag, his relaxed grin still visible within the fog that he exhaled. Prior to this moment, I'd seen him light plenty of smokes. But this time, I watched in sheer horror as he flicked away his ashes.

And he did it all without a hint of guilty conscience.

"Pawpaw! You're doing drugs!"

Exhaling more fog, he looked down at me, struck by confusion. "Do what, Bop?"

"McGruff and my teacher says you're doing drugs! You're smoking a cigarette! You're doing drugs!"

Sometimes the truth is hard to swallow, and Pawpaw Jim denied my accusations. But deep down, I sensed he knew that I knew the truth.

So help me, McGruff.

Alas, my awareness brought with it another issue. McGruff always encouraged us to report crimes to the police or an adult we trusted. But I wasn't so sure I could rat out Pawpaw Jim. I mean, this was the friendly old man who let me ride horses and held openings for me when I needed to get across barbed wire when we roamed the countryside. He also occasionally played fun songs on the harmonica. If I turned him in, he'd be playing that harmonica behind bars.

This predicament ate me up, and I couldn't bear to look McGruff in his plastic eyes—eyes filled with disappointment.

The passing of time helped ease some of the guilt, despite Pawpaw Jim's refusal to stop using. And then one day, McGruff talked with us about fire safety and the importance of not playing with matches.

"There are people out there who start fires on purpose," McGruff noted. "They're called 'arsonists,' and they're up to no good."

This message, by far, seemed a lot less condemning compared with McGruff's other one that tormented my conscience—at least until, once again, I visited my grandparents and caught Pawpaw Jim setting fire to some brush outside, puffing a cigarette as he did so.

You think you know a person, and yet, this I did know: The old man was out of control.

My little hands were tied. I wanted to help McGruff devour crime, but I also didn't want Pawpaw Jim to get gobbled up. Without meaning to, I'd become part of the problem. I was innocently guilty.

Opelika-Auburn News
APRIL 28, 2019

BACKROAD SKEPTICISM

Under a rock with a lizard—that's where my family discovered me when I was a baby. Or so I was told growing up. Anxious to see what was underneath, my family lifted the mysterious rock and marveled at the sight of a human infant stirring alongside a frantic reptile. Naturally, my great-grandfather, Henry, was adamant on pocketing the lizard, but my mother insisted they instead take the baby.

So I was hauled away to a nice home, clothed, fed, nurtured, given a name. I was also indoctrinated into a civilized culture, in which I was taught to forego my primitive reptilian ways in favor of refined human customs, such as bathing, brushing teeth, and the trimmings of finger and toenails. These customs likewise included the mesmerizing wonder of cable TV. In fact, the glowing magic from the little box in the living room inspired me to speak my first human word:

"HBO!"

I'd hit the jackpot and won a swell life.

Of course, I was far too young to have formed any memories of my time spent under the rock with the lizard, who I assume is a long-lost sibling. For a time, I used to try to communicate with lizards I caught off the porch or behind our old country church. But it soon became apparent that I'd somehow forgotten their sacred language. Likewise, their frenzied squirms and bites were solid assurances that I was not a welcomed sight.

I reckon that was the price I paid to become civilized. Still, I sometimes question what life may have had in store if I'd stayed under the rock. Maybe I'd have ended up near some swamp or in a big aquarium somewhere, becoming agitated each time some doofus tapped on the glass. Most likely, I'd have ended up as fishing bait, though I seriously doubt I'd have helped some fisherman catch anything worthwhile—maybe a soggy boot or log, but that's probably about it.

Come to think of it, I've learned to doubt a lot of things. After all, it was part of my civil indoctrination, and I had the best teacher a young'un could've hoped for when it came to learning the fine art of backroad skepticism: good ol' Pawpaw Jim. He taught me many things, like being sure to charge by the hour when you're too young to handle a chainsaw.

Seeking firewood, Pawpaw Jim once spent over two long hours trying to down a tree that absolutely refused to fall. My job was to gather the wood he cut, and I was given the thumbs-up to clock-in for the job the moment he cranked the saw. Pawpaw assumed the old pine would fall in no time. And his major miscalculation earned me some easy money, as I was instructed to wait nearby until the tree was down.

Afterward, I learned to be very skeptical—and often appreciative—of Pawpaw's time estimates. But the old man's best lessons were usually given during rides in his pickup.

A young Pawpaw Jim Sanders guards his
mother, Reoma, against varmints.

It was along country backroads that Pawpaw's musings gave rise to my own reservations about the legitimacy of the weatherman's forecasts or whether a swift kick to the gut by a horse would truly be enough to convince Mawmaw Sue to postpone some farm chores. I still doubt the latter.

These backroad schoolings also included qualms about whether a cup of coffee could be genuinely cherished without cream and sugar, as well as the need to pray for those with opposing political views. I still doubt a divine intervention could truly help anyone with a preference for coffee minus creamer, regardless of their political affiliation.

But what I remember most about these backroad schoolings was the pop quiz, during which Pawpaw would abruptly point to a random spot along the roadway and announce with excitement, "Hey, did you see that deer over yonder?"

Not wanting to disappoint, I'd instantly remark, "Yep, sure did."

Expecting him to describe a mighty buck sporting a jillion antlers, Pawpaw's voice would suddenly lower, his tone disappointed. "I didn't see no deer," he'd say, frowning. "There was no deer there. Why'd you lie?"

Sometimes I'd shrug and embrace the guilt: "I don't know." Other times, I'd say I thought I'd seen something that looked like a deer. On other occasions, when it was obvious Pawpaw's glasses badly needed cleaning, I'd stand firmly by my fib, insisting, "But there was a deer over yonder! I seen it! I did see it!"

If I played this tactic just right, Pawpaw could be moved to express a genuine sense of error: "Oh, okay ... my bad! Maybe there was a deer over yonder, and I didn't see it."

Looking back, I now understand that the old man was only trying to make sure I didn't go through life like some gullible chameleon, attempting to blend in with things without questioning the legitimacy to it all. "Don't be afraid to ask questions," Pawpaw taught me, no matter the source—even if the source was him.

The old man left his mark. He's to blame for my questioning people's bold declarations and eyesight, preferring instead to focus on people's actions, as well as whether they're any good at playing games like darts. Only thing is now, when I challenge him, Pawpaw Jim plays the victim card, remarking with sincere curiosity, "Why do you always have to be so skeptical?"

Maybe I should just go back under that rock.

Opelika-Auburn News
JULY 7, 2019

THE FRONT PORCH: A TRUE SOUTHERN WONDER

No matter where I go—Grandmother's house, a barbecue joint, the DMV to renew my license—I long for a front porch to park my rear. It's my comfort zone, my sanctuary, the place where I can unwind and reflect, ever so deeply, on life matters, big and small. A good cup of coffee or cocoa facilitates the process, as does having a good rocking chair and a good companion, who's prone to sharing their own musings—or chewing on some gossip, good ol' rich, tantalizing, fatty gossip.

If ever there was a patent on front porches, surely it included a section or footnote about its being a chief instrument for sparking verbal—and by extension, physical—warfare. Truly, there is no deadlier weapon, as a front porch grants front-row access to virtually all Southern theatrics, especially in small towns.

A porch dweller may, indeed, live many miles away from a given bout of drama. But rest assured, those sitting on a much closer porch will always catch sight or wind of the spectacle. And soon, very soon, every porch may as well have been "the" very one where everything—raging arguments, juicy affairs, fist-fighting duels—went down.

Guilty until proven innocent? Bless your heart, friend. This and similar assumptions aren't welcome on the front porch. And if they somehow happen to sneak by and take a seat, they're shoo'ed away via side-eye scowls and subtle, though highly condemning, remarks: "But, y'know, that boy/girl ain't never done right."

Nope, not even the time they delivered to you that crucial stick of butter or loaned you those couple of dollars; nor the time they stopped to help you change that flat tire or gave you a lift—none of those times matter, as long as there's some delicious gossip to chew on the front porch.

Of course, it's not all negative. Some things are sweeter than any traditional glass of Southern iced tea. There are declarations of true love; wedding and birth announcements; the send-off of a soldier and a warm "Welcome home," family gatherings; the sharing of recipes, fishing, and hunting stories; and remedies from old wives' tales. There are gatherings of pea shellers; the soothing sight, smell, and sounds of rainy days; comforting views of blooming spring flowers, fall leaves, and seasonal yard decorations; the hypnotic tinkling of wind chimes.

It's all there, all on the front porch, where many life lessons are taught as well. It was on a front porch that Pawpaw Jim showed me how to relay my worries over to the Good Lord in prayer. It was also on a front porch where Pawpaw assured me that God already knew who was going to be my wife, long before I knew myself, he added. At the time, my mid-teenage mind was certain it already knew this answer. But it was wrong. That means God and Pawpaw Jim, I reckon, were right.

Then there are lessons that are learned the hard way, like the lesson one of my kinfolks was given when he thought he'd gotten big and bad enough to not only take on his daddy but win the fight. His wiry old man, however, debunked this belief, knocking his ornery son out the front door and onto the front porch.

Stupefied, the son got up and charged back inside the house, refusing to accept what had just happened. But his daddy gave him an instant refresher course, and the poor, stubborn son found himself knocked back on the front porch again. That time, the lesson sunk in pretty good.

Other lessons simply come at random, devoid of any—or very little—foreshadowing. One I gained happened when I was about four years old. I was out playing with an orange cat on the front porch of Uncle Leon and Aunt Emma Sue Sutton's house. Rather, I was trying to play with the orange cat. It refused to come out from under a chair.

After trying unsuccessfully to lure the cat out, I finally got down on my knees and lunged for it. In return, the hissing cat swiped my forehead, and I went inside to show Uncle Leon.

"Which cat did that to you?" he asked, examining my wound.

"The orange one on the front porch."

Uncle Leon nodded. In the most deeply sincere voice I'd ever heard from a grown-up, he asked, "Want me to spank him?"

I remember thinking he was only kidding. Grown-ups said things like that all the time.

Grinning, I nodded. And that's when Uncle Leon got up, went outside on the front porch, and grabbed hold of the cat. He kept his word.

That day I learned that some old men don't play. They really do mean what they say. The proof was indisputable, right there on the front porch.

Opelika-Auburn News
NOVEMBER 10, 2019

LOVE KICKS FROM THE STICKS

Rain, sleet, or Earth-rattling lightning bolts, Slim promised to meet her out by the creek that evening—anything for his sweet darlin'. Naturally, Slim's younger brother, Spark Plug, tagged along. The two roamed the countryside together during those old Depression days, seeking mischief and finding it just fine. But on this particular evening, Spark Plug was itchin' to meet his teenage brother's girlfriend, who was rumored to be a genuine, breathtaking goddess.

Of course, this rumor was started and circulated by Slim, and Spark Plug figured he might as well check her out. After all, if things didn't work out between the two love birds, maybe she'd fancy someone a tad younger.

This notion was instantly dismissed the moment Spark Plug laid eyes on Slim's goddess, whose enchanted beauty must have seriously expired. Perhaps she'd lost a bad bet with Sasquatch and took on its features—that or the poor gal traded it all for a gigantic glob of plug chewin' tobacco.

"Come here, S*hh*lim," the goddess beckoned between spits, her packed mouth slurring some of her talk.

Horrified, Spark Plug watched as Slim complied, eager to reach his prize. The goddess stretched her neck and stood on her tippy toes, lips puckered.

Spark Plug walked on home, leaving the love birds to their business. No doubt, true love is legally blind, he figured.

— *A Lovely Gamble* —

Blind it may be, but that didn't stop true love from creeping up and blindsiding an unsuspecting Magnificent Margaret, whose legendary tale of courtship has gone through some stretchin' over the years. Here's one version of it.

Magnificent Margaret's special surprise came after "Round Town Ronnie" fell hook, line, and sinker for Cutie Susie. These two could hardly wait to make their union official at the courthouse, and Susie implored Magnificent Margaret to ride along and share her excitement.

Unbeknownst to Susie and Margaret, Ronnie asked his pal, No Excuse Bruce, to join them as well. Naturally, No Excuse Bruce considered several reasons why he couldn't go, given how he was eager to stake some more of his luck in stud poker. But he kept all these excuses to himself when he gazed upon the gorgeous Magnificent Margaret, whose alluring magnificence rendered him spellbound.

Although they barely spoke during the ride to town, Bruce was certain of his destiny. He had an eye for Magnificent Margaret. That's why he followed Ronnie and Susie into the courthouse.

This was Bruce's one shot, his biggest gamble. Poking his head out the door, he called over to Margaret, who waited by the truck: "Hey, what's your name?"

Startled, Magnificent Margaret told him. She asked why he wanted to know.

"Because we gonna get hitched too," Bruce said.

His dopey grin made her laugh. They stayed married 'til death they did part.

— *True Love vs. Pete* —

It seems nothing can stand in true love's way. My old friend, Pete, would have begged to differ.

The proof was undeniable after Pete grounded his teenage son, James, from driving one weekend. Defiant for the sake of love, James bowed out his chest, sneered, and declared he was, too, going to drive. He had a big date that Friday night.

Keys in hand, James made his way out the front door to the white '66 Chevy.

Alerted to the rebellion, James's mother sounded the siren—"Pete, he's leaving!"—and Pete rushed out the side door. The pickup vrrroomed, shifted into reverse, and started backing out to turn frontward and head down the driveway.

But Pete leapt onto the front bumper, determined to keep his word.

Alarmed and amazed by his daddy's sheer tenacity, James watched as Pete held on, steady as a pro bull rider. Pulling the hood's latch, the old man reached inside and snatched the coil wire off the engine. The pickup died as it rolled.

Poor James suffered a terrible case of lonesome heartache that night. All because true love, despite attempting a bold getaway in the Chevy, just couldn't prevail against the likes of ol' Pete.

Opelika-Auburn News
FEBRUARY 3, 2019

HEARTBEATINGS

Heart attacks run strong in my family—strong in quantity and magnitude. No one sharing my genes will dispute this fact. In fact, if we find out you're kin, we're likely to warn you—in a heartbeat—about this artery-blockin', chest-wrenchin' assassin.

Just ask Aunt Gaye Harcrow, who used a jar of mustard to fight off her attacker. That's because, at the time, she thought she was only having a really bad case of heartburn. And a remedy for easing heartburn, according to wisdom imparted by Aunt Gaye's mother, Mawmaw Muggie, is swallowing about half a finger-dipping's worth of mustard.

For three days, Aunt Gaye and her jar of mustard were inseparable. It was her only defense against shortness of breath and the invisible massive weight that squashed her chest. Mustard eased the pain during the first two days. But the remedy proved absolutely futile by the third night, and Aunt Gaye struggled to find a comfortable place to rest: her bed, her recliner, her couch. Wherever she went, the mustard jar followed.

On the morning of the fourth day, Aunt Gaye's best friend of thirty-five years, Alice Holland, insisted she go to the hospital. But Aunt Gaye refused.

"I ain't goin' to no hospital for no heartburn," Aunt Gaye declared, fearing embarrassment. Absolute, she dipped her finger in the jar for another dose.

But her friend persisted, and soon Aunt Gaye was driven to the emergency room, where a doctor asked her who her doctor was. All her life Aunt Gaye had always been the one to stop what she was doing to help take others to see a doctor, declining to go see one herself.

That's why she told the emergency room doctor, "I guess you are. You're a doctor, aren't you?"

I'd bet good money that confused man's heart skipped a couple of beats. Accepting his nomination as her official doctor, the fella tended to Aunt Gaye and made sure she got some rest.

Her mustard jar, in the meantime, sat nearby on a nightstand by her hospital bed.

Nevertheless, when she left to go home, Aunt Gaye's daughters assured their mama that she wouldn't need any more of that old remedy: "You've got medicine to take now."

— *Flock of Terror* —

As for my great-grandmother, Reoma Sanders, she tried to keep her heart attack at bay with aspirin. Of course, I'm surprised those little white pills hadn't turned to dust in that old bottle at the time, given their prehistoric expiration date.

Luckily, my grandmother was able to bounce back. But that certainly almost wasn't the case on another occasion, when her heart nearly burst from extreme fright.

This happened many years ago, when she and my great-grandfather, Henry, were on vacation, and they pulled their car over for a rest. They'd parked by a big field, where a gigantic flock of large, watchful birds had stopped for a rest as well. Ever so tenderhearted, my grandmother reached for a pack of cookies.

Sensing what she had in mind, and having watched Alfred Hitchcock's movie *The Birds*, my grandfather warned her not to do it. But she did. Extending a cookie in one hand and holding the pack in the other, my grandmother walked steadily toward the birds, calling to them, "Here, birdies!"

She didn't have to call them twice. The birds engulfed her, their flapping wings mirroring her flailing arms. Screaming in terror, she managed to dash back to the car, where her poor tender heart desperately needed to recover.

In the meantime, my grandfather was desperately trying to recover from his own reaction to the whole thing. He'd nearly died from laughing.

—— *Head and Heartache* ——

Some folks may say that that incident was no laughing matter, nor was the time I nearly had a heart attack of my own when I was a little kid.

At the time, I'd been playing in the backyard, where we kept our pet bunny, Butterbean.

The black rabbit looked like a jumbo-sized chocolate treat, and he certainly had enough speed in him to keep a good distance between him and any child hyped up on a major sugar high. Still, I couldn't help but repeatedly try to grab ahold of him, reaching as far into his cage as I possibly could on each attempt.

But I regretted the time I finally got him, as his hind feet scratched my arms and caused me to jolt upward, hitting my head extremely hard on the cage's doorway. Pulling back, I rubbed my aching head, and as my hand began to drop, I saw it: blood. In no time at all, my hair felt soaked.

Running back to the house, I found Aunt Stacey, who was watching over me and my sister that day. I held my arms over the spot where my head hurt and whined for her to pay me attention. At first she assured me that everything was all right, lifting my arms to have a look.

However, upon looking, her eyes filled with fright. My whole cotton-top noggin was crimson. "Oh my God!" she exclaimed, and my face mirrored her panic as my heart leaped up my throat.

A quick wash and further inspection of my head showed I wasn't going to die or need stitches. It was only a little gash. But it still took my heart a little while to fully grasp this.

Opelika-Auburn News
OCTOBER 27, 2019

EVERYONE IS MEANINGFUL TO SOMEONE

My father is known for his cheerful smile and contagious laugh. Rarely will one carry on a conversation with him and not be subjected to both, as he can discern the sheer irony and humor in most scenarios. Nevertheless, he absolutely beams any time he speaks of "Daddy," my late grandfather, Pawpaw Buck Huffman.

Between the 1960s and 1990s in rural Pickens County, you could have watched Buck pass by on his motorcycle, perhaps a late-model 1940s Harley-Davidson or an attractive Honda CB750, as he likely wore a helmet too small for his head and stylish sunglasses that concealed his striking blue eyes. He would also most certainly be wearing denim bib overalls and laced-up brown boots, the left heel of which required adjusting to accommodate the length discrepancy of his legs.

"That leg got shorter every time Daddy held it up to show me," said my father, Mike "Doe Doe" Huffman. "That leg was shorter, but it was mostly shorter in his head."

My father cherishes his memories of his daddy. Vivid and fascinating, the stories he can tell of Buck range from comically amusing to profoundly intense, while depicting a man who embraced a unique existence. They also depict a man who undeniably made an enduring impression on my father, one which enhanced his understanding and compassion for others, regardless of their reputation.

As a teenager, my father lived in a country home in Gordo with Buck, behind which Buck had once grown three towering marijuana plants in a former hog pen. One afternoon, a helicopter flew over their residence twice, rousing Buck's paranoia. Fearing the arrival of law enforcement, Buck hurriedly called a friend over to haul away and keep his plants. My father insists the helicopter was merely a random coincidence.

Incidentally, the first movie my father watched in a theater was Cheech and Chong's *Up in Smoke*. Assuming he had taken his son to see a cartoon, Buck emerged from the theater once the film ended and declared, "Hell, all they did was smoke dope."

Another of my father's memories consists of a story told to him about how a youthful Buck once saved some money, bought a pair of leather dress shoes, and rode a bus to New Orleans. Spending his remaining cash on liquor and women, Buck returned to Pickens County approximately one week later, the soles of his new shoes completely worn out. "He had to do a lot of walking and hitchhiking," my father said. "I imagine his feet were mighty sore."

When my father was deployed to Saudi Arabia during the Gulf War, he received a letter from Buck that assured him: "Son, I love you more than I did any of my ex-wives."

Given his daddy's divorce rate, my father instantly remarked, "Lord, Daddy, I hope so!"

Other memories include how my father and Buck rode motorcycles together—untamed spirits with routine early bedtimes. Mostly, however, my father recalls how Buck overcame his alcohol addiction to get custody of his children. Visiting their daddy every other weekend for years while living with supportive relatives whose finances became strained, my father and his sister were nearly taken by the state.

My father remembers the magnitude of Buck's addiction: how he gulped down whiskey despite painful stomach ulcers; how he once became so drunk that he crawled to the refrigerator for another beer; how he'd drink rubbing alcohol if desperate. For his children, Buck quit—cold turkey. "You can't change the past, but you can make things better," my father says. "And he did."

Buck's professional background primarily involved dusty sawmills. The only land he ever owned was his burial plot. My father affectionately describes him as an "ordinary man," one who recognized life's essential elements and never hesitated to tell his children, "I love you."

To my father, that was plenty.

Everyone is meaningful to someone, regardless of a person's past, social status, personal values, and approach toward life. My father acquired this insight during his youth, as he learned how to look beyond exterior impressions and detect others' redeeming qualities. Such an outlook continues to characterize his love and perception of his daddy. When asked what he misses most about Buck, my father's response is brief and poignant: "Everything."

The Birmingham News /AL.com
SEPTEMBER 20, 2015

Pawpaw Buck Huffman with his young'uns, Mike and Stacy, in the 1970s.

DOE DOE OF ARABIA

Three little old buttons, bright and cheery yellow, are pinned to an equally aging red-and-white ghutra that hangs reverently in my garage, beaming slogans that inspire feelings of pride and triumph.

IN SAUDI ARABIA MY DADDY IS A HERO

GOD BLESS MY DADDY IN SAUDI ARABIA

WELCOME HOME DADDY

I was two back when my 20-year-old father, Mike "Doe Doe" Huffman, joined the Army National Guard in 1988. It was something he'd always wanted to do, always wanting to be a part of something bigger than himself.

The Army welcomed all 145 pounds of him.

After a swearing-in and a salute, my father was shipped out via bus to Fort Jackson, South Carolina, where he and other fresh recruits were greeted by the loud, grating voice of a drill sergeant.

In fact, right before my father left for basic training, my great-grandfather and Korean War veteran, Henry Sanders, gave him the heads-up: "Now, Mike, I'm gonna go ahead and tell you, the one thing that's gonna get you is your laughin'. You laugh at everything."

And that's exactly what my father did shortly after getting off the bus, as the poor fella standing next to him in line was being called every synonym to "scum," "worthless" and "disgrace." The recruit agreed, repeatedly yelling, "YES SIR! YES SIR!"

My father tried to hold it in. But all he could think of was Gomer Pyle, at least until he felt the brim of the drill sergeant's hat pop him in the forehead, and he became acquainted with the most vicious pair of bulging eyes he'd ever seen.

Instantly, my father took up right where the other recruit left off: "YES SIR! YES SIR!"

For eight weeks, my father understood this was no laughing matter, especially when the female drill sergeant took over and made it her mission to make every push-up, sit-up, rope climb, obstacle course and heart-pounding hike even more strenuous.

She hated men. There was no doubt. Snarling in disgust, she never let the recruits forget they all smelled "like a bunch of goats."

Eight long weeks.

After basic training, my father spent a few months learning the fine art of auto mechanics. However, rather than repair vehicles, he found himself behind the wheels of flatbed trucks once the Gulf War got underway in 1990.

Being handed the truck keys didn't surprise my father at all. Since high school, he knew his destiny would roll along life paths on eighteen wheels. So it was only a matter of time until the Army recognized his special talent and put it to good use.

Before my father and other soldiers were deployed, the town of Gordo and city of Reform held parades in their honor. Driving a deuce-and-a-half truck, my father was steering toward the crowd gathered in downtown Gordo when his daddy, Pawpaw Buck, leapt onto the driver's side door and grabbed my father's arm, riding along.

The old man was squalling.

"I gotta go, Daddy," my father said, gently shooin' the old man away as the cheers got louder. "I gotta go ..."

So off he went, flying out of Fort Benning, Georgia, and landing in Saudi Arabia. Then he and the rest of his unit, the 946th

Supply Company, headed deeper into the desert, where the blazing sun and shade competed for sweat. The shade always won, inflicting an Alabama-like humidity upon anyone who got in it.

In fact, the dry heat was so intense that, after washing clothes in a bucket and hanging them out between tents, they'd be dry in about two hours. Cool breezes were always welcomed, but strong winds brought blinding sandstorms.

These were among the things my father got used to while hauling supplies and equipment to various units throughout the desert. But one of the most memorable sights came while driving toward the outskirts of Kuwait, when he gazed upon a massive cloud of darkness.

The entire area underneath was engulfed in a smoky haze.

The phenomenon was the result of arson committed by a retreating Saddam Hussein and his troops, who turned multiple Kuwaiti oil fields into an inferno.

The grimness was made even grimmer by the sight of starving Kuwaiti children, inspiring my father and his traveling comrades to toss out MREs (Meal, Ready-to-Eat) to a group of kids they encountered along the roadway.

Completing his duties, my father was happy to get back to glorious Alabama and his family.

"Are you gonna have to go back?" Pawpaw Buck asked him.

My father reckoned he'd have to if he got the call.

"Naw, you ain't puttin' me through that again, Doe Doe," Buck assured him. "They don't take one-legged folks."

My father insists he didn't do anything special during the war. But I disagree. When our country needed a trucker, he was ready to ride.

My father was Doe Doe of Arabia.

Opelika-Auburn News
JULY 5, 2020

STICK, BOOT, AND OTHER PROUD NICKNAMES

Outfield. Deep, *deep* in the outfield. That's where my Little League coach always sent me. And that's exactly where I always played in the grass and dirt, facing opposite from the game my fellow Little Leaguers were playing.

"I ain't coming back," Pawpaw Buck Huffman said as he watched his first—and, indeed, last—game during my youth baseball stint. "He's ruinin' the Huffman name!"

Laughing, my father remarked, "Daddy, we ain't *got a name!*"

True. Coming into the world with a surname you don't have to worry about smearing has its perks. It was kind of like driving an old, banged-up and rusty car you never have to wash or worry about denting. We're just happy the ride still cranked.

Maybe our last name wasn't glamorous, but Lord knows my folks took a lot of pride in the nicknames given out. And that's a fact on both my father's and mother's sides of the family.

Take, for instance, my cousin "Stick," who can thank her daddy for her lovely title. To my knowledge, there is no awe-inspiring backstory behind it. The name just naturally popped into her daddy's head as he looked upon her when she was a baby: "*Shhh*ttt*ickkkk*!"

In fact, her daddy called her this so often that, for a time, her own pawpaw didn't know that her actual name was Kayla. And now her family has welcomed a new member into their circle: "Twiggy."

Of course, some folks are given nicknames long before they get their actual name. This was the case for my maternal great-grandfather, Henry Alfred Sanders, whose birth certificate identified him as "Baby Sanders." His parents had many children, and I reckon they just couldn't come up with an official name for him. So everyone just took to calling him "Junior," at least until he enlisted in the military when he turned 18.

My grandfather was told he *had* to have a real first name before he could join. As a result, he afterward told his family he was "Henry," the same name as a gentleman who'd made quite an impression on him when he was a young'un. And so Henry was "Junior" no more, except to his brothers and sisters.

Another endearing nickname belongs to my father, who's been known his whole life as "Doe Doe." This is yet another name that was randomly given out. And absolutely no one, other than close family members, had any earthly idea whom I was referring to when, as a child, I gave my father's actual name, when I answered the question, "Hey, boy, who's your daddy?"

"Mike Huffman."

"Who?"

"Doe Doe."

"Oh! Buck's boy!"

That's right; my father was Pawpaw Buck's young'un, Ol' Buckaroo. His real name was Adolph, but everyone knew him as "Buck." That's because, as you've probably guessed, he was absolutely buck wild.

This was a man who once saved a chunk of cash, bought a new pair of leather dress shoes, and then grabbed a bus ticket to New Orleans, where he spent the rest of his money on every wild time the city had to offer. Penniless, he had to walk home to Alabama, hitchhiking when he could. It took about a week, but he finally made it back home—minus the soles of his worn-out shoes.

My siblings have nicknames as well. My sister, Hannah, goes

by "Boo Boo Shay," which started as "Bubala," a Jewish term that refers "to any person that is considered darling and close to one's heart," according to urbandictionary.com. Boo Boo Shay has two sons, Hayden ("Big Mane") and Ryder Roo Roo.

But I reckon my other sister, Brittany, has the simplest nickname of all, one that hold its own with "Stick." Her nickname is "Boot."

And then there's my youngest brother, Tristen, who goes by a variety of names: "Tric," "T-Bird," and sometimes just simply "T." My father used to call him "Water Bug," referring to my brother's tendency to be everywhere and literally into everything. "He's just like a water bug," my grinning father would declare. "Just turn on the light, and watch him go."

Lately, my father and Tristen call each other "June Bug," or just "June." "Hey, J*uuu*ne! Watch out, and let a real man show ya how it's done, June!"

My other brother was given the name "Boog," a shortened version of "Booger Rat." These days he's called by his first name, Matt. Still, I remember the good ol' days of "Da Boog."

Naturally, I was unable to tiptoe past my family's nickname department. I even gave out a few of them, like the one that belongs to my wife: "Sweetie-Poo." I also dubbed Aunt Stacey as "CiCi," given I couldn't say her name right as a toddler.

But once upon a time, I was called "Homeboy Doo." That was decades ago, and I remember the name went through a couple of trimmings: "Homeboy" and then "Homer." None of these really stuck, not like the nickname I've carried nearly all my life: "Ol' Big Keith."

I've been told I'm called this because I can use big words and, allegedly, come up with big ideas and big plans. Or maybe I'm just a big mouth. I also weighed practically nothing as a child. Now, my weight fluctuates. Big Keith can get even bigger if he doesn't watch it.

Yessiree, my folks cherish a fine nickname, and I wondered

what my son, Kaleb, would be called after he was born. It didn't take long for my father to answer that question.

"Ol' Big Kaleb!"

Now that makes a Huffman proud.

Opelika-Auburn News
APRIL 14, 2019

BURNING RUBBER WITH MOTORCYCLE OBSESSIONS

The streetwise hellions peeled out, motorcycles roaring, dark shades and leather jackets defying the blinding sun and icy gusts. Fierce. Reckless. Always craving action. The unruly duo zoomed through the streets, drawing stares, stealing hearts, and prompting mutters of disgust.

Individually, they were stout enough to intimidate the rowdiest among rebels, routinely shattering others' confidence in fistfights and street races like jagged stones hurled through plate glass. United, they were practically unstoppable. So opportunities to expand into a trio or more were naturally appealing.

That's why, on this particular day in the 1970s, the duo rolled up the driveway and onto the front porch of a small rental home, revving their bikes wildly at the front door to beckon a third member outside. For a moment nothing stirred, so they revved louder and longer.

The door finally opened, and out shuffled a frail old lady. She shivered from the cold and fright. Silence instantly replaced the deafening madness, and the roughest of the two meekly asked if their fellow biker was home.

"I think he moved up a couple of blocks," the old lady said, motioning with an unsteady finger.

"Thank you, ma'am."

"You're welcome, sonny."

Egos deflated, the streetwise hellions puttered away.

This is one of many stories involving bikers that I've soaked up over the years, as my family has been obsessed with motorcycles for generations. The love is dear and deep. Pawpaw Jim, ordinarily compliant with Mawmaw Sue's daily commands, flatly defied her order to stay out of the local dealership. He now rides a Kawasaki Vulcan 750, retired and carefree—even when the varooming reminder of his disobedience renews Mawmaw's scorn.

My other pawpaw, the late Buck Huffman, always wore a helmet far too small for his massive head. Proudly steering a Harley-Davidson along country roads in the 1960s, Buck rode a red Honda CB750 by the time I knew him. And regardless of distance, whether one hundred or an even quarter of a mile away, Buck routinely fetched a rag from his leather saddle bag to wipe his ride. She always shined—as did all of my father's bikes. These days he takes to the streets on a green 1996 Harley, often joining others on benefit rides to battle cancer or deliver gifts and donations to children in need during the holiday season.

A young Pawpaw Buck and his country ride.

Wherever he goes, a little American flag flaps behind him, gloriously.

My father's life involves two passions—truck driving and motorcycling—and he's willing to share the joys of both with anyone remotely interested. When it comes to motorcycles, however, he makes one thing absolutely clear: The bike comes first.

One of his lady friends learned this the hard way, years ago, after begging to try out his new Kawasaki Vulcan, the one he'd bought straight off the showroom floor. Following behind her in his pickup, my father watched helplessly as she suddenly veered off the paved road and onto a gravel one.

It was like watching the whole thing happen in slow motion, my father said, and there was nothing he could do. Instantly losing control, his lady friend went flying off to one side of the road as his precious bike flew the other way, landing in a ditch.

Instantly stopping his pickup, my father raced past his friend to aid his true love. Upon reaching her, he frantically called out, "Help me get her up out of this ditch!"

Carefully wheeling his injured beauty to safety, my father looked to his friend. Blood dripped from her elbows and knees. "You okay?" he asked.

Her reply was none too friendly.

Of course, I have far more pleasant memories riding as a kid with my father. Seated behind him as a passenger, my arms propped at my sides or around his waist, I absorbed all the rapidly moving sights and sounds. We'd ride in a pack or just the two of us on his bike, cruising about everywhere we went: around town, through Tuscaloosa, or even to Mississippi. Long travels tested the endurance of your back, and the winter wind would sometimes make your teeth chatter, despite a good jacket and jeans. It didn't matter. We were loose on the highway, the roaring engine expressing our delight.

Opelika-Auburn News
NOVEMBER 25, 2018

SILVER BULLET: A TRAGIC LOVE STORY

Friends, let me tell you, the more time you spend looking at things like Rorschach inkblots and optical illusions, the more you start to see peculiar sights everywhere. Some sights are easier to detect than others, depending on things like lighting and how elaborate a given image may be. But more and more lately, I've been noticing a variety of amusing caricatures, hieroglyphics, and patterns on everyday objects and thingamabobs.

Take the granite countertops in my kitchen. I can't tell you the number of times I've spotted a cartoonish face or critter staring back at me as I sip my morning coffee. Once I could have sworn I saw Ivan Pavlov, the Russian physiologist who famously conditioned hungry dogs to salivate at the sound of a bell.

Other images—spooky jack-o'-lantern expressions, bizarre snowflake patterns, etc.—have emerged on the tile flooring, as rust spots on gadgets, and from finger and nose prints on windows, compliments of my young son and vigilant cats.

Chip crumbs in a bowl are open to interpretations as well, or the whole chip itself, like the Cheeto I nearly ate that was shaped like a shark. Likewise, mustard and barbecue stains on shirts can bear striking resemblances to butterflies or airplanes, or a preschooler's depiction of a two-headed armadillo wearing a straw hat.

There's also the sticky residue from the tag I removed from the cats' water bowl, which at times looks like a gorilla. Or perhaps it's an elephant?

Your guess is as good as mine. But there is one thing I've seen consistently. This I can say without a speck of doubt.

Most folks who come across my father may only see a middle-aged trucker who prefers to dwell on the few ups life has dealt him, always snubbing his nose to the ever-present (and ever-increasing) downs—a former spring chicken, who, despite having had his fair share of feathers plucked over the passing of many seasons, still never misses a chance to strut around the coop. But when I look at my father, I see a black and silver 1979 Ford F-150, a breathtaking beauty of a truck that flaunted her glorious name across the top of her polished windshield.

Silver Bullet.

My father succumbed to her enchantment the very moment he set eyes on her, long before she was even for sale sometime in the early '90s. From the start, she called longingly to him, practically blowing kisses and batting her long lashes, from her spot on another man's yard in our little town.

His heart aching with unquenchable yearning, my father waited, and the second he saw she was looking for a new home, he didn't hesitate. He rushed to the bank for a $3,000 loan and brought his babe home.

And, buddy, she was a sharp babe, radiating black and silver ecstasy everywhere she roamed, on marvelous tires that were always bejeweled with glistening rims. Her interior was a palace: black and silver upholstery, including a black dash with wood trim; full seat; three-speed on the column; and an air conditioner that always gave a steady flow of perfumes the smell of fresh spring air, summer breezes, fall festivity, and winter wonderland. Insert a Lynyrd Skynyrd or Guns N' Roses cassette in the stereo, and you're Sweet Home Alabamin' your way to Paradise City, *vrrr*ooming in style via the exhilarating rumble of a 302 engine with a four-barrel carburetor.

This was how things were for my father and his precious Silver Bullet for nearly two decades. They were a lovely pair, destined for one another, and everyone who waved to them as they rolled through downtown knew it.

True, she only gave 15 miles per gallon, making it tough on the wallet during trips to places like Florida. But she always got my father where he wanted or needed to be—especially to work, even when his job was across the state line in Mississippi. And wouldn't you know it, she was always waiting for him when he got off, regardless of whether it was payday or a period of financial fasting. Their love was genuine.

Their love was so genuine that it ignited envy among other men, whose lustful desires impelled them to approach my father, all shifty-eyed and shady, to ask: "Hey, Doe Doe, you lookin' to sell that truck? How much you take for it?"

As if you could put a price on true love—this sentiment gnawed at the yearnings of many seekers. But it absolutely gobbled up our late cousin, Jerry, who was relentless in his own pursuit of the stunning Silver Bullet. And his bargaining was most intense when he was entrusted with performing critical operations under the Bullet's hood anytime anything went remotely amiss.

For many years, my father repelled his cousin's attempts to seal a deal, refusing to defy his one true love—that is, until cruel fate put a short in the motor's wiring, and Jerry was the only country mechanic who could keep her running. Plus, there was her gas mileage, which kept shifting more and more in Jerry's favor.

Finally, to the shock of all who knew him, my father stopped listening to his heart and swapped keys for a red and black Chevy S-10. It promised him about 25 miles or better on gas.

The sad day my father watched Silver Bullet leave his driveway left a tragic scar on his spirit. The scar became even deeper when he later learned that, after undergoing more trading, Silver Bullet met her demise when she collided with a tree.

But I remember the first time my father passed by Silver Bullet and Jerry on the road. Steering his Chevy, my father refused to look at them, keeping his gaze focused forward on his lane. I don't think Silver Bullet looked at him either.

Neither could bear to see the other with a new partner. Theirs was a hard break-up, plain for all to see.

Opelika-Auburn News
NOVEMBER 24, 2019

Silver Bullet and me.

P-O-T-A-T-O

All because he wouldn't take that darn thing out of his mouth.

That "thing" was a little Aspirin box, measuring about one and a half inches long, and it was filled with matches, each of them broke off a bit so they'd fit. Pawpaw Buck Huffman had the little box sticking out of his mouth, refusing to listen to his school teacher's command: "Boy, take that darn thing out of your mouth."

Aunt Betty Jean, Buck's five-years-younger sister, watched quietly with the rest of her fourth-grade class as the tug-of-war got underway. It was 1949, and a 15-year-old Buck was in the fifth grade. He and his little sister shared the same classroom and teacher at the little schoolhouse in the Zion community, located approximately ten miles from downtown Gordo.

Of course, Aunt Betty Jean got to go to school far more consistently than Buck, who helped their daddy with his work, cutting down timber. Ol' stubborn Buck probably wished he had been in the woods with his daddy that day, especially when the teacher stuck a finger in his mouth and tried to force the little box out.

The teacher tugged with her finger, causing Buck's leg to act out of reflex (of sorts) and promptly kick her. Hard. It was the last time he ever went to school—all because he wouldn't take that darn thing out of his mouth.

It sure put Aunt Betty Jean in a spot. She was afraid their teacher was going to take frustration out on her. She definitely felt this way after a spelling test, when the teacher told her to stand up from her desk in front of the class.

"Spell 'potato,'" the teacher instructed.

Aunt Betty Jean felt the pressure. All eyes and ears were focused on her.

"Potato," she said. "P-O-T-A-T-O. Potato."

Silence. Nodding, the teacher said, "Betty Jean, you are the only one in the whole class who spelled 'potato' right."

Relieved, Aunt Betty Jean sat back down. She was happy to know she was a spelling genius, although she couldn't shake off the nagging suspicion that her teacher must have thought she'd somehow cheated. Still, she handled the pressure well and triumphed.

Spelling tests will do that to you. Believe me, I know. I've felt that same damning pressure, the kind that all but guarantees your world will come crashing down if you add a godforsaken "e" at the end of "potato," "tomato," or "tornado."

My mother made this very clear many years ago, back when I was in the second grade and had a big spelling test coming up. I was a very, very, very hyper kid. I was a spider monkey of sorts, or so I was told—one powered by an unlimited amount of raw energy. Had my parents been engineers, they could have built a power-generating contraption with a giant hamster wheel for me to run in, helping us save hundreds—if not thousands—of dollars on power bills.

Alas, my parents weren't engineers, and all my poor mother wanted was for me to just sit still, stop bouncing around, and study that darn spelling list. But spider monkeys, especially the ornery type, don't care a thing about spelling lists.

And yet, my mother pressed on, convinced there *had* to be a way to tame the instinctive hyperactivity of a sugared-up spider monkey. All efforts seemed futile, at least until she finally said something that managed to get the untiring creature's attention: "Boy, if you don't pass this spelling test, you're gonna regret it."

Very briefly, I paused, actually feeling those last three words sink. I resumed my spider-monkey ways, but there was definitely a minor easing up in my hyperactivity, the reading on my internal energy meter lowering from "full blast" to "semi-full blast." It seemed to correlate with the fluctuation of my mother's words, emerging back and forth from semi- to total consciousness: "Gonna regret it."

The intensity of her warning nagged me, its pressure mounting as each day drew closer to the dreaded spelling test, inspiring me to periodically glance briefly at my spelling list. Every word seemed much longer and more complicated each time I reviewed them.

Finally, doomsday arrived. All my classmates sat at their desks, anxiously awaiting the moment our teacher would look down upon us and call out each gruesome word. My heart pounded. It was spell or fail time.

Holding her dreaded list, our teacher called out a single word, pausing momentarily. She repeated the word and then gave us a little more time to write our spellings down. Closing my eyes, I gulped. This was the end.

Suddenly, something happened. All the pressure that had seemed absolutely certain it was going to crush me, echoing in its sinister guarantee that I was "gonna regret it," lifted. I felt my brain turn on, and I could feel the vast multitudes of various gears and sprockets activate and churn out not only spellings but the right spellings.

P-O-T-A-T-O.

It was as if I had the whole spelling list engraved under my eyelids. My confidence soared, scoring me a one hundred.

Relieved, I sat quietly at my desk. I realized I wasn't "gonna regret it." It was a feeling of sheer survival, of having defied some of the greatest odds imaginable in the kid world, and that has stuck with me to this day, giving me the reassurance I desperately need each time I sit down to write anything.

Oh yes, I'd triumphed, though my nerves certainly suffered for it—all because I wouldn't just sit still and study that darn spelling list.

Opelika-Auburn News
MAY 10, 2020

SPLINTER: EVERY CHILD'S WORST NIGHTMARE

You've been there. We all have. When you're a kid, it's one of the most agonizing hells you can ever survive—hands down. I'm speaking, of course, of those ill-fated times when a splinter got stuck in a finger, spurring the most extreme magnitude of excruciating pain imaginable. We're talking the kind of pain that always inspired genuine pleas for mercy, knocking us to our knees as we held a poor, puffy-red finger up to God Himself, praying for a cure.

When a cure came, usually in the form of a no-nonsense grown-up armed with wicked-lookin' tweezers or fingernail clippers, we'd hightail it out of there, content with our misery for a little while longer.

Thoughts of my own encounters with these small-but-deadly monsters surfaced recently during a visit home, while I was out jogging and spotted one of my kinfolk, TJ. Instinctively, I threw up a hand to wave. And that's when I felt the strangest twinge in my ring finger. It was trying to tell me something, trying to remind me. Sure enough, I remembered.

Early elementary school. The playground. I was romping around with other kids on some old wood equipment, smiling and laughing, brimming with innocence, when it happened: A massive splinter, one that had to have been the size of a full-fledged popsicle stick, got stuck in my finger.

Time stopped, as did my feet as I stared with growing alarm at the terrifying piece of wood that invaded my skin. Rapid thoughts swirled like laundry in a spin cycle: *Oh, Lord, why?*

Why me? Of all the blasted kids on this playground—heck, in this school, or even in the whole wide world—why did it have to be me?

Looking back, I reckon it could have been chalked up as pure coincidence. Possibly, and yet I'm still haunted by a nagging feeling that it happened because I'd lied about a buddy in class, claiming it was he who snuck in a carton of chocolate milk to drink and then spilled it on some classroom puzzles while trying to be all secretive. In truth, we both concealed our cartons on the way back from the lunchroom. But my fellow smuggler abruptly decided he was going to take his home.

I, on the other hand, soon realized that karma—that boomerang-like thing my mother always warned about—never turns a blind eye to any misdeed, regardless of age. Everyone is fair game.

This realization dawned on me as a group of other kids surrounded me, our collective telepathy sounding the alarm that something was terribly wrong. All eyes were on my poor finger.

"Awww man."

"Ooooo! That's a biggun!"

"Can you still move your finger?"

I could, but it most definitely hurt. Someone suggested the teacher be told. But this remark was instantly met with a few shushes, including my own. Telling the teacher meant the tweezers. There had to be another way. It needed to come quick.

This was life or death.

Suddenly, there was an abrupt parting in the small group, and a confident TJ emerged. He grabbed my hand, inspected the damage, and then looked me in the eyes.

"Hey, man, I can get that out," he said. "My daddy's a doctor. I can get that out."

Now, this was before I knew TJ and I were kin. Otherwise, I

would have called phony-baloney, just like the girl next to me did: "TJ, your daddy ain't no doctor!"

"Yes, he is! He showed me how to handle these sorts of things."

TJ must have gotten a failing grade in splinter removal. He most certainly did that day. Because that doggone thing got much deeper.

"Awww, man! I'm sorry!" TJ wheezed, his confidence now totally defunct. "I guess you are gonna die."

There was zero doubt. It was either the dreaded tweezers or a slow, painful death. Neither of these options, arguably, was remotely better than the other.

The kids around me dispersed, off to enjoy the remaining time outside with their non-splintered fingers, leaving me to my grim fate. I kept to myself the rest of the day, at least until Mawmaw Sue Sanders picked me up after school and noticed my fixation on my finger.

"Oh, you've got a nasty splinter," she said. "Looks pretty deep too."

My heart raced again. A grown-up knew my secret, meaning unbearable torture was guaranteed. I knew I was about to embark on a whole new emotional roller coaster, one with no height requirement.

Expecting the tweezers, I felt relieved when Mawmaw Sue emerged with her sewing kit. My relief was short-lived, however, as she pulled out a small needle. The light hit it just right, and Mawmaw Sue seemed to admire its sinister glint.

"Give me your hand," she said, then addressed my hesitancy, assuring, "It won't hurt. I promise."

Now Mawmaw Sue had never lied to me—never, ever, except when it was absolutely necessary. Still, on that day, I'm proud to report her words didn't manifest into any lie bumps on her tongue.

Applying years of expertise in mending ripped clothes and making cherished dolls, Mawmaw Sue kept a steady grip on her needle and labored like a bona fide surgeon, ever-so-gently slicing through layers of skin to make a lifesaving incision. In practically no time at all, the splinter was gone.

A doctor she was not, but Mawmaw Sue came through, and I reckon that'll do.

Opelika-Auburn News
JANUARY 19, 2020

LOVE TRIES ... AND SOME THINGS ARE JUST MEANT TO LAST

"Don't touch that phone."

This was directed to my father, who stopped in his tracks and looked over at Pawpaw Buck. The old man leaned forward in his recliner, eyes alert, convinced that a certain someone was trying to make contact.

Again.

"She already won't stop calling me," Buck grumbled. "It'll make things worse if you answer. Don't you dare pick up that phone."

My father dared to pick up the phone.

Loud and grating, the voice on the other end didn't hesitate: "*Where you been*, Tiiiiger??"

They say, "Love will find a way." It certainly tried that day. And for several days afterward, my father referred to Pawpaw Buck by the name that love ever so graciously bestowed upon him: "You need anything from the store, Tiger?"

I reckon it could have been worse. Ol' Buck could have been waving to the prettiest girl from his kindergarten class while balancing on one leg on a shopping buggy at the dollar store, only to have the wobbly thing flip over and spill all its contents on him. Or he could have become filled to the brim with puppy love upon discovering a letter from his third-grade crush under his desk, only to be told moments later the message was meant for someone else.

Love tries. But I reckon sometimes it just doesn't try hard enough.

If love would've used a little more elbow grease in Pawpaw Buck's marriages, then the old man could have expressed himself a bit differently than the way he did in an old letter he wrote to my father, back when my father was deployed to Saudi Arabia during the Gulf War: "Son, I love you more than I did any of my ex-wives."

Love ought to know by now that it's got to put a lot more *oomph* into these relationship deals if they're truly going to spark up good and last—we're talkin' the need for some major league commitment, the kind that latches on like a snapping turtle who refuses to believe that thunder exists. Storm all you want, that ornery joker ain't lettin' go.

That's right. We're talkin' the kind of commitment where you interrupt the middle of class to ask your high school teacher if you can be excused to the restroom, only so you can hightail it down the hall to your sweetheart's class to address the note she slipped you earlier, the note that questioned whether the love y'all shared was truly meant to be.

This was the case for Pawpaw Jim Sanders during his senior year in 1967, when he'd set his sights on Sue Ann Bitler, the most beautiful gal at Lancaster High School in south central Ohio. Their love blossomed shortly after a classmate asked Pawpaw Jim if he could give Mawmaw Sue a lift to her job at a local supermarket. Pawpaw Jim didn't mind, but Mawmaw Sue almost didn't get in for the ride. Convinced no one their age could possibly own a sharp muscle car, she thought Pawpaw Jim was stealing that midnight blue '65 Pontiac GTO.

But the car really was his—honest!—and after finally convincing Mawmaw Sue that the cops wouldn't come looking for them, Pawpaw Jim became her devoted chauffer from that point onward. As payment, he received pearly white thank-yous and heart-melting goodbye waves—keep the change, of course.

In fact, Pawpaw Jim enjoyed giving Mawmaw Sue rides to work so much that he even bargained with the school principal and assistant principal to get out of detention. This happened after a lunchroom fight erupted, and the principals reckoned a paddling each day for a week would suffice. Pawpaw Jim agreed, although he ended up joking around with the principals in their office all week and then got all five whacks on the last day.

But it was this level of commitment that kept getting him dates with Mawmaw Sue. She was, after all, the woman of his dreams. In fact, long before Pawpaw Jim even met Mawmaw Sue, he dreamed of marrying a beautiful, hardworking woman with gorgeous blonde hair. Only, his dreams wouldn't let him get a good look at her face. But after gazing into Mawmaw Sue's lovely hazel eyes, Pawpaw Jim knew. Anytime he got around her, it was breathtaking, and his heart raced so fast it bordered on a full-fledged heart attack.

Talk of marriage soon followed. This, however, was followed up by a major dissenter.

Henry Sanders, my great-grandfather, believed the two were too young to get hitched. He wanted his son to go to college, an opportunity he wished he'd gotten back when he was a young buck in West Alabama, and he gave his honest opinion to Mawmaw Sue's mother, Erma.

Erma, in turn, gave her honest opinion: "Oh, I think they're all right."

The matter reached a standstill. But the impact from the objection was felt, prompting Mawmaw Sue to write Pawpaw Jim a note. She didn't want to upset his family. Moments later, Pawpaw Jim was standing in the doorway of her math class, telling the teacher he needed to talk to Sue Bitler.

The two married in the chapel of the city's First Methodist Church on August 6, 1967. They drove away in Pawpaw Jim's GTO, the words "Watch Ohio Grow" written on the top of the car in white shoe polish.

Pawpaw Jim never could get those words to wash off. Some things are just meant to last.

Opelika-Auburn News
FEBRUARY 16, 2020

Pawpaw Jim and Mawmaw Sue Sanders on their wedding day, August 6, 1967.

I'VE KNOWN HER ALL MY LIFE

I've known her all my life—and yet, I don't know who she is. Of all the numerous people I've met and befriended, I feel that she is the one I should know best: vivid highlights of her childhood experiences, her dreams and fears as she aged, details of her proudest and darkest moments.

Granted, I do know some of these things, but only because I was there when they happened. Beyond these moments, however, I'm afraid I cannot share many stories that offer a rich depiction of who she was before I came along. It's not necessarily her fault; I've simply never asked.

My mother taught me many vital lessons that I strive to live by, and for that I owe her a debt of gratitude that I'll never come remotely close to repaying. But it would be nice if I could occasionally reflect on, or perhaps even share, insightful stories from her youth.

These thoughts settled on me as Mother's Day neared. What began as a brainstorm of ideas about what my son and I could do for his mother suddenly shifted to reflections of my own mother. I thought about what she means to me, and how her words and actions helped mold my understanding of the world and the many kinds of people who dwell within.

And then something else dawned on me. It was an older realization, one that emerged the day my son was born. But now there was more clarity to it: My son will learn from me ... and much of what I can teach came from my mother.

I knew what I had to do. Like an eager knowledge-seeker embarking on a sacred journey to gain wisdom from an omniscient guru perched atop the peak of a towering mountain, I set out to learn more about my mother. As I did so, I also reminisced about some of the experiences she and I shared throughout my early youth, as well as the lessons she imparted.

* * *

My mother turned 18 about a month after I was born. I certainly don't remember, but I was told I was among those on the bleachers as her graduating class received their high school diplomas. People walking around just kept stopping to coo and look at the baby, Mawmaw Sue Sanders said. Chuckling, my great-grandmother, Reoma Sanders, insisted Mawmaw Sue was the one walking around and proudly showing off her three-month-old grandbaby.

My mother and father got married at the start of their senior year. A picture in an aging red photo album shows them smiling and standing together by a table with two candles and trays bearing sandwiches, nuts, chips, mint candy, and a white wedding cake decorated with blue-frosted roses. My mother wore a slim white dress, and my father, a white dress shirt, trim baby blue suit, and tie.

High school sweethearts—somehow their love managed to blossom despite the inappropriate letter my father gave my mother to express his initial interest. She told him off, she said. And he later apologized and said he shouldn't have talked to her like that. The letter had featured the kind of things that typically fill a teenage boy's mind once hormones ransack all reason, leaving impulsive lust to fend for itself. Nevertheless, my mother promptly assured my father she was not that kind of girl.

In a photo from my own wedding album, my wife and I hold hands as we stand smiling among friends and family who tilt sparklers in our direction. Holding a bouquet of flowers, my wife is gorgeous in her white, lacy dress, a deep purple sash tied around her waist. My charcoal suit, white dress shirt, and purple tie are quite snazzy, but they pale immensely in comparison to the striking woman wearing the lovely outfit next to me.

Several memories suddenly flashed as I gazed at the picture: holding doors open for incoming ladies; making chairs available when all others were taken; lifting and carrying heavy items. My mother stressed the importance of these things throughout my life, and she assured me that if I wanted to get a good woman and keep her, then I'd better talk to her like I had some good home-raisin'.

Admittedly, my chivalry has become quite rusty. It began gathering dust and moss around my late teenage years. However, I'm well-aware that my wife would be hitched to someone else if I'd used an approach like my father's.

Of course, being respectful and courteous does not appeal to all women. I remember holding a door open for one of my dates, and she rolled her eyes before passing through and snarling, "You don't have to do all that."

"Yes, I do," I retorted. "My mom said so."

* * *

She wanted to make others pretty. As a little girl, my mother fixed her dolls' hair and did their makeup. She soon transitioned to her friends and younger sister. She was convinced that becoming a beautician was her life's calling—until her parents discouraged her. Beauticians don't make a lot of money, they said.

Less than three months after I turned 11, I told my mother I wanted to be a writer. I know the timeframe is right because I dated my first short story, "Hooch the Pooch Learns that Dogs Can't Fly."

"I want to write a book," I told my mother. "Just like the ones in the library."

"Go ahead then," she said. "Worst thing they can do is tell you 'no.'"

I remember writing several short stories about my dog, Hooch.

Among his many adventures, he daringly escaped a ruthless street gang of vicious canines. He also rescued a turtle and even managed to get himself married before fathering a litter of little Hooches.

After I handwrote the stories, I was able to get them typed before redrawing my illustrations. My mother took me to the post office, and we mailed the manuscript to a publisher in New York. The wait was long, but I eventually received a rejection letter in the mail. Hooch the Pooch didn't meet the publisher's needs at the time.

I showed my mother the letter. And that's when I learned the value of persistence and being willing to take risks. "At least you know you tried," she said.

I knew, someday, I'd try again.

* * *

One day at school, a much older and very round kid teased my mother, saying her nose made her look like a witch. My mother started to counter with a remark about his weight, but he cut her off: "I know! I already know what you're gonna say!" Words can be mighty hurtful.

A broken heart is a whole other pain.

My parents divorced when I was nine. Before then, I can remember many nights when my mother would wake me and tell me to get in the car. We were going to try to find my daddy.

My little sister was likely sleeping in the back as we rode through the countryside. I remember feeling tired and anxious while peering out the window at the surrounding darkness. We'd pass peoples' homes and occasionally a chicken house. Sometimes the headlights of other late-night drivers would appear and go by.

My father may never be a "one-woman" man. My mother realized this, and she suddenly found herself confronted with two life paths: bite her tongue and maintain an oblivious facade or end the marriage. The path she chose was primarily guided by her concern over how things were affecting her children.

Many years have passed, and my mother said talking to my

father is now like speaking to any other ordinary person. Their marriage began well, but things soured after my father returned from Saudi Arabia, where he served in the Gulf War with the Army National Guard. My father said his greatest regret in life was losing his marriage to my mother. If he could go back and change things, he wouldn't hesitate. "She was a damn good wife," he said. "And a damn good mother."

My mother loved my father, and I witnessed how her world crumbled. But I watched her steadily rebuild as well. Gradually, her blue eyes lifted as her genuine smile returned.

Mawmaw Sue once tied a carburetor to a push mower with a shoestring to keep it working. Through her own strong will, resourcefulness, and faith, my mother regained her happiness.

"Be willing to forgive," she said. "But remember what people are capable of doing."

* * *

My mother's favorite songs as a child ranged from "Jesus Loves Me" to "It's a Small World" and the theme for the Mickey Mouse Club. She'd also sing anywhere: at home, school, Sunday school. Singing brought her joy, and she's embraced it all her life.

My favorite songs included the themes for the *Teenage Mutant Ninja Turtles* and *Ghostbusters*. But I'll never sing Nicole C. Mullen's "Redeemer" with the same loveliness and sheer passion as my mother. Many times I've watched as she's taken the stage and stirred people to their feet, hands clapping or stretched trembling toward the ceiling, their eyes gleaming with welcomed tears.

Like her work ethic, my mother takes great pride in her singing. Just as her dependability reinforced a previous boss' willingness to loan her extra money for Christmas to buy presents for her children, my mother's voice continues to prompt others to request for her to visit a church and grab the mic.

"Always strive to be your best," she said. "And keep the welcome mat out for all of life's blessings."

They may sound simplistic, but many of my mother's lessons prove to be complex and challenging when put into action. This thought surfaced and faded as I recently watched my toddler son use a sand-bucket shovel to swat at bubbles blown his way from a plastic machine.

My mother wanted to be a beautician, myself a writer. My son may want to be a bubble exterminator, but he still has a good while to make up his mind.

My son will learn from me, and much of what I can teach came from my mother. *I'll try*, I told myself. *And I'll do my best to teach him—just as you did with me, Mom.*

AL.com
MAY 14, 2017

She's been there for me all my life.

FLIRTING WITH TROUBLE

To this day, decades after being spotted, she denies any wrongdoing. But my mother was caught holding a cigarette at Dairy Queen.

This happened when she was a teenager in the mid '80s. She and my father were hanging out with some of their schoolmates in the Dairy Queen parking lot, and everybody was busy puffing cigarettes—everybody except my mother, or so she claims. She was only holding one for a friend.

And that's exactly what she told Pawpaw Jim the moment he suddenly appeared in his pickup, catching his darling daughter red-handed. "Get in the truck," Pawpaw Jim said, flicking away the butt of his L&M. Mawmaw Sue, riding alongside him, took a long drag from hers and shook her head in disappointment. How, exactly, did they manage to raise such a heathen?

"It's not mine!" my mother cried. "I'm just holding it for a friend!"

But Pawpaw Jim's deep voice got much deeper. He meant business. "In the truck. Now."

Mouth zipped, my mother complied, leaving behind her friends and the cigarette she'd held, all cool-like, between her fingers. Everyone watched as Pawpaw Jim's truck headed homeward, their smokes reappearing from behind their backs.

My father, who'd gone to the restroom right before the whole thing went down, returned shortly afterward and noted my mother's absence: "Lawd, where'd that crazy girl run off to?"

She was at home, getting rehabilitated via some serious grounding, my friend.

Some folks, it seems, just can't sit still long enough to stay out of trouble. Especially during that hopelessly rambunctious and utterly confusing period of life we all know as youth, when tendencies to flirt with trouble rise to phenomenal peaks.

Take my father, who, like his ancestors and offspring, was certainly no saint. As a teenager working in chicken houses and earning chicken scratch, he couldn't afford a new tag for the old Ford Falcon his daddy gave him. But that was only a minor inconvenience, mind you.

My father loved flirting with trouble.

No tag, no problem, he figured. Squirting syrup on the plate, he next applied a fistful of dirt. He then hit the road, aiming for downtown, in a ride the color of lemons.

The old car drove like a lemon too. Lacking rear shocks, it bounced everywhere it went: *K-tunk! K-tunk! K-tunk!*

Come across a pothole and the bouncing got much worse, prompting those riding along to ask my father to pull over for a minute: "Man, I can't get a swig of my drink."

This went on for about a year, giving that old ride plenty of time to attract lots of attention. After all, my father did everything he possibly could to keep that ride washed and wiped clean—everything except the license plate, of course.

But never once was he stopped by a pair of flashing blue lights. Nope, the fun stopped when the car finally died, tuckered out from all that bouncing around.

No ride meant my father had to tone down his infatuation with trouble, at least to a degree. Of course, I'm not fit to judge. I, too, flirted plenty with trouble during my teens. Once, a friend and I elected to sneak a whole pizza—box and all—into a movie theater. Ordering the greasy Italian pie and then popping into a nearby shoe store to ask for an extra-large bag, we next got in line to buy our tickets. I can't recall what movie we wanted to see, but

I do remember how all the corners of that pizza box bulged in the snug bag. It was blatantly obvious what we had in tow.

We reached the ticket taker, who looked sternly at the two of us and then at the bag. His eyes repeated this sequence a couple more times. Mine did similarly.

There was a brief pause and then, at last, the guy waved us forward. The previews had just begun, and we sat in the back, devouring slices of pizza that tasted like sweet victory. We'd flirted with trouble—and gotten away with it.

Opelika-Auburn News
FEBRUARY 17, 2019

EXCUSES, EXCUSES

Zeke and Haywood were ready. At long last, after spending a week's worth of eternity waiting, Friday afternoon had finally come. And if the fuse was lit just right that evening, then Friday night was guaranteed to be a blast.

This meant everything—the selecting of clothes, the shining of shoes, the combing of hair and the generous splashing of strong cologne—had to be perfect. Otherwise, the women folk downtown would fancy some other hotshots.

The fellas pulled off perfection in record time.

All was going well, at least until it finally came time to give a good excuse for heading out and leaving their wives at home. In fact, their wives might have believed them—except no one goes fishing dressed in their Sunday best on Friday evening.

The fact that they also plum forgot their fishing poles as they started heading down the road didn't help matters, either.

I reckon it's true when folks say not all excuses are created equal. Some can certainly be shot down much easier than others. My great-aunt, Juanita, or "Nita" as her siblings affectionately called her, learned this the hard way long ago, back in the mid-1940s, when she was around 16 years old.

At the time, she'd gone on a date with a fella who drove a little ol' car, one that was at least capable of carrying them back and forth to downtown Gordo. There was no need for any fancy ride. As long as it rolled and got her out of the house, Nita was happy. If the driver was handsome, that was a bonus.

On this particular day, Nita deemed her date irresistibly good lookin', and so they made plans to celebrate their puppy love under the moonlight. The only problem was Nita's daddy, Pawpaw Lee Makelin Huffman, expected her home by nightfall.

No doubt, she made it home in time. But now she needed a good excuse to go back outside to her date's car. Its engine rattling and trunk facing the front of the house, the car shared the driver's itch to head back down the driveway.

Nita didn't waste time.

Her excuse groomed and ready, she opened the door to Pawpaw Lee Make's bedroom and called to him. The old man was lying on his bed, getting ready to drift off to sleep, but Nita had his attention. She told him she and her date needed to ride back into town to pick up her older brother, Cecil. She said they'd seen him earlier, right as they were about to head to the house, and it would certainly be a shame if poor Cecil was unable to hitch a ride and had to walk home so late. Her bleeding-heart date reckoned going back was the right thing to do too.

Pawpaw Lee Make listened to all this, soaking it in. And when his darling Nita finished, he raised up out of bed and walked to the front door, where he reached for his shotgun that hung over it.

Nita stood behind her daddy, eyes now wide open, fear squashing all of her new dialogue to gibberish. She thought she'd done a good job delivering her excuse. It was definitely one of her best performances. What she didn't know was Cecil had already come home about an hour or so earlier and went on to bed.

Now their daddy was standing in the open doorway, his shotgun aimed at the back of the waiting car. Slinging gravel like sparks, the old ride launched down the driveway the moment the buckshot hit it, vanishing in a thick cloud of dust.

Poor Nita—a shame her brother didn't have enough good sense to go along with her good excuse.

Opelika-Auburn News
APRIL 26, 2020

JAILHOUSE SHENANIGANS

Damn leg just won't stop shrinkin' …

This, Pawpaw Buck Huffman was convinced, was certainly the case—no need for any tape measure, no point diggin' out the old yardstick. The proof was plain to see, even from the finger-smudged lenses of Buck's aging bifocals, each time the old man threw up his legs to compare. That one leg just kept getting shorter than the other. It was simply a little piece of reality he had to accept.

Now, Pawpaw Buck's left leg truly was a couple inches or so shorter than his right—blame it on the Huffman genes. That's why he had a nifty heel lift on his boot, to help give more balance to his shuffle. Let's just say that boot did its best.

But Pawpaw Buck was no stranger to exaggerated paranoia, particularly when it came to his physical well-being. Since the day he was born, the man was certain each day he lived was surely going to be his last. Still, if a number of random health complications or a gruesome traffic accident didn't take him out, then surely that doomed leg was going to nag him to death.

"Look here!" he'd say to practically anybody sitting nearby. And then up those legs would go, the left forever overshadowed by the right. And that shadow just kept getting bigger. Or at least it did in Buck's head.

In fact, that leg once got him tangled up in some serious jailhouse shenanigans. This happened around the early 1950s, back when a young Buck roamed Pickens County in search of wild times and even wilder women.

Naturally, it was mandatory that these weekend adventures involve plenty of hard liquor, a fact that often resulted with Buck recovering from hellacious hangovers inside Gordo's old jail. If he didn't come home by Sunday evening, then Buck's daddy, Pawpaw Lee Makelin, knew there were at least two spots he'd likely find his son: the two cells inside the old jail.

My great-grandfather, Lee Makelin Huffman, with his son, Pawpaw Buck.

But this time in particular, the police arrested an innocent Buck, shortly after he'd finished his shift at the sawmill and grabbed his paycheck. Eager to embark on yet another wild weekend, Buck made his way on foot to the bank. But his lopsided shuffle, made especially wobbly by his fast pace, spurred a watchful policeman into action, and a sober Buck was put under arrest—public intoxication.

Always willing to admit when he was drunk—"Ain't no use tryin' to hide it"—Buck insisted that, this time, he really hadn't had a drop—not yet, anyway. That was just the way he walked. "You'd walk like this too, if you had a leg that wouldn't stop shrinkin'."

But the policeman wasn't buying it and proceeded to do a search on poor ol' Buck, confiscating the brand new pocket knife Buck's daddy had given to him.

Shortly after the jailhouse delivery was made, Buck's daddy, Pawpaw Lee Make, caught wind of the matter—word spreads like the plague in small towns—and went to check on his son. The old man promptly raised hell upon discovering the police had, indeed, arrested a sober Buck, who was soon set free.

The problem now was Buck's treasured pocket knife was deemed "lost." The arresting officer claimed he couldn't find it. So the police chief went right out and bought Buck another one.

—— "Ain't you supposed to be in jail?" ——

Of course, Pawpaw Buck wasn't the only one in my family to gain experience from some jailhouse shenanigans. Take, for instance, a shenanigan that involved my great-great-grandfather, Alfred Sanders, who helped build Gordo's old jail—and spent a few nights in there.

Now, Alfred was known locally as an all-round handyman, especially when it came to roofing and painting. It was believed that he could paint up a hole in a barn, and he likely plumbed every building in town. So, naturally, he was an obvious pick for helping put the jail together.

The town sure appreciated it. Alf did too. By helping build the jail, he would know how to get out of it.

This became apparent shortly after one of his stays inside Gordo's iron suite. I reckon the room service wasn't anything worth bragging over, as Alfred was spotted eating at a nearby café.

Naturally, this raised the eyebrows of those who knew about his arrest.

"Alf, what're you doing in here? Ain't you supposed to be in jail?"

Nodding, Alfred swallowed a bite and assured that all was well. "I just got so hungry I had to get something to eat," he said. "I'm gonna go back when I'm done."

I reckon some jailhouse shenanigans can give you a leg up when it comes to filling a big appetite.

Opelika-Auburn News
MARCH 29, 2020

DEAL 'EM

Two dollars—that's how much cash my great-grandfather, Henry Sanders, was handed by his daddy, Alfred, one Friday afternoon. My grandfather was around 10 at the time, and he was told to go downtown to buy two dollars' worth of hamburgers for his daddy's card game that night. This was during the Depression, back when hamburgers in the downtown area near where they lived cost a nickel apiece.

Forty burgers—this request raised the eyebrows of the burger joint cook.

"You sure that's what you want?"

Absolute, my grandfather nodded. "Yep."

"Aww right, then … order up!"

The burgers filled two large paper bags. My grandfather carried them home, hurrying along but being careful not to drop anything.

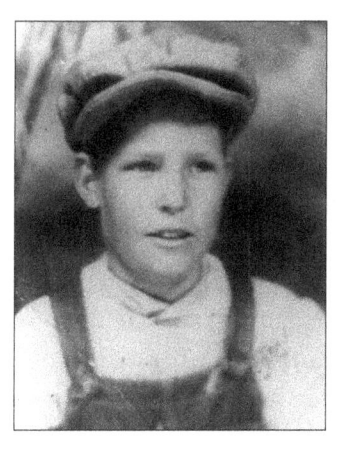

A young Henry Sanders.

Card night was a serious affair at his parents' home. And this level of seriousness attracted some serious appetites.

May as well feed 'em. May be the last meal some got to eat for a while, depending on the hands they were dealt. Still, regardless of the cards he got, one thing was certain: My grandfather's daddy would "win" back his two dollars.

Watching his daddy deal, fold, and win was my grandfather's earliest exposure to playing cards. And this fascination stayed with him and his generation for the rest of their lives.

I remember well, as a kid, how my great-grandparents' house would be filled with family, friends, and some folks hardly anybody knew on weekend evenings, all of them aiming to shuffle a few decks and get dealt as many winning hands as possible. The room where everyone gathered was gray, not from any paint or wallpaper, but all the cigarette smoke that swirled into a great fog. And yet, no one lost sight of their cards. Some never lost sight of others' cards either.

Games were played at two round tables, during which everyone got caught up on the latest family drama, while betting against one another. Often, poker chips were used. Other times, visitors carried tin boxes or wore fanny packs full of coins. And by the end of each game, you could tell who was riding high on a lucky streak. They jingled louder wherever they roamed.

Win or lose, everyone was convinced everyone was cheating. And this outlook sparked many heated confrontations:

"Doctor says my short-term memory isn't too good. It's gettin' harder to remember things. But I know for a fact I'm not losing my mind, and I know full well I did not renege. I did not renege!"

"Yes you did, Henry! I ain't no liar! You did renege!"

When things got too heated, one or more of the maddest would huff away from one table and join those playing at the other. The game may not have matched the one they left, but it didn't matter.

Poker? Spades? Blackjack? Go Fish? "Whatever. Just deal 'em."

I witnessed many epic showdowns. But few rivaled the competitive intensity of those between my grandfather and his sister, Lorene.

Inheriting the stern face of their mother, my grandfather's and Aunt Lorene's mugs were unreadable—especially Aunt Lorene. No one, absolutely no one, could read her. And my poor grandfather suffered for it. Try he certainly did, but he rarely dropped a winning hand against Aunt Lorene.

It wasn't so much that she had a knack for winning, but rather the condescending calmness of her gloating: "Now, Henry, don't make such a fuss. No need to get all worked up. Let's play again, and maybe you'll win."

At this point her mocking grin would appear. Besides her usual poker face, it may have been Aunt Lorene's only other expression. And that's when she'd add, rasping, "Maybe."

His face becoming redder with his sister's every word, my grandfather would reshuffle the deck. His icy glare stayed locked on his grinning sister, and his bifocals slid down the bridge of his nose. His nostrils flared.

But Aunt Lorene only smiled, revealing her pearly dentures. And eventually, when he'd finally had enough, my grandfather would shove away from the table and stomp upstairs to his bedroom.

Feigning innocence as she basked in her glory, Aunt Lorene would look around at those nearby, saying, "Now, why does he always get so mad at me?" And then her mocking grin would reappear.

Nosey, I'd creep upstairs and peek inside to spy—or check—on my grandfather. And there he'd be, lying atop the blanket on his bed, staring at the ceiling. From the record player nearby, Hank Williams sang of his own sadness.

Aunt Lorene had done it again. Unlike his daddy, my grandfather couldn't even win back two dollars—nor enough change to buy a nickel's worth of hamburger meat.

Opelika-Auburn News
MARCH 3, 2019

My great-grandparents, Reoma and Henry, could never resist a good card game.

COUNTRY ENGINEERS

Wood scraps and 1-by-6 boards—*check*. Bolts and angle iron—*check*. Steering wheel, two red wagon wheels and two more wheels off an old-timey push mower—*check*. Gas-powered engine from an old Maytag washing machine—*check*.

Looks like we've got everything we need. Now grab the toolbox.

It's time to get creative.

Of course, there's no need to tell that twice to a seasoned country engineer—someone who's never stepped foot inside a fancy college but can fix, rig or build practically anything. Creativity comes natural to them, in exactly the same way it comes to genius mad scientists, driving their bizarre ambitions.

Only difference is a country engineer's lab is normally a garage or backyard shed.

This was the case for my great-grandfather, Henry Sanders, who made a go-kart for his children in the mid-1950s. Many years ago, Maytag washing machines ran off gasoline, offering a nifty solution to my grandfather's need for a power source for his contraption.

Put together the other pieces of the puzzle and voilà! You're ready to take off in a homemade hot rod, one fully equipped to putter around the yard at a blinding speed of 3 miles per hour, the engine roaring with fierce intensity: Putt-Putt-*Pow*!

Just like an antique John Deere tractor.

Pawpaw Jim Sanders takes his little brother, Louis, for a ride on the homemade hot rod in the mid-1950s.

All you needed was an adult or someone heavy enough to kickstart the thing and off you'd go, easing to a halt only when you pulled the special lever by the steering wheel. The lever acted as a clutch, and pulling it caused the whole engine to slide backward a few slots, or a couple inches, toward the rear axle, shortening the distance between the pulleys on the engine and axle and relaxing the fan belt.

That's technical country engineering gibberish that basically means the go-kart would brake until you released the lever.

In fact, the only way to turn the thing off was by snatching the wire off the spark plug. Of course, this was an impossible maneuver for a four-to-five-year-old Pawpaw Jim and his little brother, Louis, neither of whom could reach back far enough. Plus, if you failed to grab the insulated part of the wire, you'd be guaranteed some serious shock treatment. That's why Pawpaw Jim and Uncle Louis would drive around their family's house in circles, yelling for someone to hurry up and come to their assistance: "STOP THIS THING! WE WANT OFF! WE'RE TIRED!"

It was either that, or wait for the thing to run out of gas.

Although it could hold about a pint, the hot rod gave excellent mileage. It was practically indestructible as well, enduring things ranging from the time Pawpaw Jim collided with the chicken coop out back, to the time my great-grandfather drove it up a massive hill to test the engine.

He figured the thing would eventually give out. But all the way up the little ride went ... and kept on goin'.

Putt-Putt-*Pow*!

Now, if you're riding around with that kind of power, you might as well figure out a way to give it a little more speed. That's exactly what my great-grandfather tried to do one day while his wife and kids were gone to church. But by the time my grandmother, Pawpaw Jim and Uncle Louis came home, they saw my poor grandfather had a splint wrapped around a finger. He'd broken it after reaching back to turn the hot rod off, brushing his finger against the flywheel.

Now, another pro country engineer is Mawmaw Sue Sanders, who's no stranger to enduring the blistering summer heat while taking apart and reassembling a dryer on the fritz. This usually happened when the heating coil in her old dryer from decades ago would go out, and Pawpaw Jim would be out of town for his job.

Of course, Mawmaw Sue didn't need no man, and her keen obsessive-compulsion to get her daily chores done wasn't about to let some trivial thing like a lack of finances to make a repair call get in her way. Driven by her instinctive bull-headed grit, Mawmaw Sue learned how to resurrect the dryer anytime it died—or, rather, when it *tried* to die on her.

Mawmaw Sue is a natural at working miracles, but her finest moment was when she tied the carburetor back on the engine of a push mower with a shoestring. If she'd have had the right bolts, she'd have used them. Instead, she tapped into her country engineering instinct and did what she does best.

Improvise.

Come to think of it, Pawpaw Jim isn't a shabby country engineer himself. Several years ago, after I inherited an antique 1930s Royal typewriter, I discovered the drawband, or string that allows the carriage to move when something's being typed, had dry-rotted.

These days, folks can simply Google a remedy. Back then, however, my best bet was to show the thing to Pawpaw Jim and hope for the best. He recommended replacing the old string with some fishing line, then helped install it. Today, the typewriter still works perfectly.

All thanks to some good ol' country engineering.

Opelika-Auburn News
MAY 24, 2020

JOY OF PEOPLE

I sprung from the town of Gordo, a wee plot of West Alabama acreage in Pickens County, found smack-dab somewhere between Tuscaloosa and Mississippi. Home of the Green Wave and less than 1,700 people, it's exactly where I encountered many charming folks with bounties of captivating tales, personal accounts, hearsay, and otherwise. Absorbing every rich detail, I spent my childhood listening, envisioning, and writing.

Eventually, my fascination with ordinary people inspired me to seek out many of the local legends I'd heard so much about in Gordo, Pickens County and surrounding communities. Every one of them lived up to their expectations: World War II and other generational heroes; former pro baseball, football, and boxing athletes; a man who flew legendary Crimson Tide coach Paul "Bear" Bryant to recruiting ventures, circling the landing field a while as the houndstoothed Bear sat among other card players in the back and laid down winning hands, much in the same glorious fashion as his receivers who dove swiftly into end zones.

I'll never forget the retired high school football statistician who stored away his 30 years of notes about a two-time state champion team that no longer exists. Reminiscing about multiple yards, passes, and punts scribbled meticulously within each rubber-banded season stack, the stat man's pride in his team equaled the cherished bond of a family.

And, of course, there was the clever fella who, as a wild child in the 1980s, relied on steady chairs and milk crates to make mind-blowing shots around pool tables, while routinely hustling humbled adults amid gathering crowds inside a game room at a long-gone drive-in. Having tragically lost his father and brother to a house fire, the nine-year-old hustler found solace and pride in skillfully pocketing balls before bettors curious or foolish enough to take him on.

All of them were great pleasures to listen to. Go ahead and add David Housel, Auburn Athletics director from 1994 to 2005, to that list. Himself a native of Gordo, Housel's acquaintance represented one of my New Year's resolutions. The man is legendary where we come from, especially among those dwelling within War Eagle turfs, and I knew when I stepped foot in Auburn that our paths were bound to cross.

And so they did, recently, at Chappy's Deli. Sharing breakfast with my three-year-old partner, Kaleb, I spotted Housel and realized the time had come. Briefly excusing myself from a fabulous conversation involving Thomas the Tank Engine, I moseyed up to the nearby booth and extended a hand.

A pair of friendly blue eyes flashed, followed by a warm grin and handshake. These were all common gestures experienced during most introductions, of course, but still there was something special there that hinted of home and small-town charm. It was the all-embracing kind that welcomes new faces onto front porches or inside living rooms and kitchens for a well-spent chatter.

Chat we did, and I soon learned how we both once devoted lots of our time on the sidelines and dugouts at Gordo High School, all for the sake of newspapers and—naturally—a paycheck. While I always served as an observer, however, Housel both reported and shared the Green Wave's glory as a legitimate member of the team.

"I actually covered games I played in on the high school football team," Housel said. "I remember one night after the game going in and asking Coach Tommy White for some comments on the game, and he said, 'Well, you were out there. You played in it. You know what happened.'"

"But I will say this," Housel added. "I never once mentioned my name in the coverage of the game. I wasn't good enough to have my name mentioned."

Paid a nickel per inch as a sports correspondent for the *Commercial Dispatch* of Columbus, Mississippi, which was trying to start a circulation base in West Alabama during the early 1960s, Housel tended to write long. I did the same, though my mission was to help fill pages in the *Pickens County Herald*.

"I always hated it when they cut it, though, at the office," Housel remarked, referencing an ill-fated wallet.

The thrill of money, however, wanes when compared with the sheer magic of seeing one's first-ever byline, printed in bold ink for all to see. But the real joy dwells in the stories shared by those who trust you enough to enter their worlds. Absolutely, I share Housel's sentiment: "I think all the way through, it's always been more than yards and field goals and base hits. It's the people who get that yardage or score that touchdown, get that field goal or get that base hit. *They* are what's interesting."

Opelika-Auburn News
APRIL 1, 2018

Part 2

PORTRAITS:

SOUTHERN HEARTS, TRAGEDIES,
AND TRIUMPHS FROM
WEST TO EAST ALABAMA

GLORY DAYS: FORMER PRO BASEBALL PLAYER REFLECTS ON BASEBALL MEMORIES, CAREER WITH GIANTS

The Tuscaloosa News
JULY 4, 2017

He would stand ready on the mound, right hand firmly gripping the baseball, feeling its laces, his blue eyes locked on the catcher's mitt. He was rarely nervous. He knew, most of the time, he could just throw it by them.

Jeff Campbell knew it when he played in youth baseball in the 1950s, and his confidence grew only stronger as his pitching became even fiercer and earned him the opportunity to join the minor leagues with the San Francisco Giants.

"I guess you realize it when you start getting batters out," Campbell said. "Some people just can't get them out. But I was blessed with a strong arm, so I could throw it hard and had a good curve ball. And one of my scouting reports when I was with the Giants said, 'Not human.' Nobody that small could throw that hard. But it was just a God-given gift."

This year marks 33 years since Campbell, 73, has served as the city president of the Gordo branch of West Alabama Bank & Trust, and he is set to retire on August 1. This year will also mark

50 years since he signed with the Giants. But the best memories, somehow, seem to smell like fresh grass, leather, and dirt.

— *Cat and Mouse Game* —

Mickey Mantle was his childhood hero. Captivated by the agility and sheer talent of the home run leader for the New York Yankees, Campbell said Mantle seized the spotlight in his mind each time he put on his Little League uniform in his hometown of Gordo.

"He wore a number seven jersey," Campbell said of Mantle, "and everybody fought over the number seven. Everybody wanted to have Mickey Mantle's number."

Playing in the outfield and pitching for the Coca-Cola Bottlers, who were sponsored by the Coca-Cola bottling plant that once operated in Gordo, Campbell was never lucky enough to get Mantle's number, instead receiving the numbers two or three. Baseball was one of the few things that provided entertainment to post–World War II youth in rural West Alabama, and Campbell said he was proud to represent his team's colors of gray and red, as well as the Coca-Cola emblems displayed on the hats and shirts of their wool uniforms.

"Of course, I can tell you, in the middle of June with 100 percent wool, you were itching from the time you put it on," Campbell said. "But we took a lot of pride in playing for Gordo, and more than anything else, we had a competitive group that didn't like to lose."

Taking a field at Gordo High School, Campbell played alongside some of his closest friends: Larry Blakeney, Frank Elmore, Bobby Perrigin, and the late William "Willie" Elmore, whose father, Verdo, was a former Major League Baseball player for the St. Louis Browns during the 1920s. "We took great pride in playing for Coca-Cola," said Blakeney, sixty-nine, of Auburn, who was the head football coach at Troy University from 1990 to 2015 and also served as an assistant coach under Doug Barfield and Pat Dye at Auburn University. "We had a lot of fun. I don't know how good we were, but Jeff was pretty good."

Said Frank Elmore, 70, of Gordo, "Jeff was older than me, but he was always the guy who was going to help you out. He'd make sure whoever was going to get picked last got chosen. Jeff was a coach on the field and good-hearted. Everybody listened to Jeff Campbell. He was the leader of the pack."

Transported to games in the back of a red pickup with Coca-Cola emblems on its doors, Campbell said their team was coached by the late Travis Fair, who worked for the Coca-Cola plant, puffed cigars, and usually came to the games in crisp business suits. Removing his jacket while coaching, Fair managed the team as it competed against local rivals such as the Dr. Pepper Bottlers, who were sponsored by that soda's bottling plant in nearby Reform. The other teams, Aliceville and Carrollton, were sponsored by Lewis Lumber Company and Standard Oil Company, respectively.

Campbell said the Gordo field ran alongside a two-strand barbwire fence that surrounded the late George Koon's horse pasture. If a batter slugged a home run or outfielders failed to catch a hard line drive, then a player would raise a hand to signal that they were crossing the fence to retrieve the ball.

"Usually, we didn't have but like two balls, so it's not like it is now where they have several dozen," Campbell said. "If they hit it over there, you'd have to go get it because that may be the only game ball you got."

Reform was their primary rival, Campbell said, but he particularly remembered a highlight from a game when he pitched against Carrollton. Louie Coleman, who later became sheriff of Pickens County, coached the other team, which occasionally used a kind of secret weapon in Lewis Williams, whom Campbell estimated may have been less than four feet tall at age nine.

"They had the bases loaded, and I think it might have been a tied game, or we may have been one run ahead," Campbell said.

"And the coach at Carrollton at that time called time out, and he put Lewis Williams up to bat. And you can imagine pitching to Lewis when he was nine or ten years old. He had a strike zone 'bout like a Skoal can. Lewis would walk up there with that bat—it'd be tall as he was. He'd just stand there. Automatically he's going to be a walk. I never will forget. I said, 'If I get the bases loaded, I know who's coming to the plate.' I didn't ever want to see Lewis coming up there."

Said Williams, 70, of Carrollton, "I knew I was going to walk or strike out. I never saw the ball because Jeff would throw it so hard, but I was instructed to never swing at it. I was supposed to just stand there. Jeff was older than me, so we played on different teams. I was on the younger team, but if the older team needed me, I was there."

Throughout his youth baseball years, Campbell's passion for the game intensified, and his fast pitching caught the attention of coaches. Refining his abilities as he aged, Campbell said pitching was his "specialty" by the time he reached high school.

"As you get older, you try to develop different pitches," he said. "Curve ball and the change-up, and the fastball—and you just really try to find the best rhythm you can that you can throw those different pitches. And what you're trying to do is fool the batter. You're trying to keep the batter off balance, and it's kind of a cat and mouse game as to how you pitch."

Emboldened by green and white as he represented the Gordo Green Wave from 1959 to 1962, Campbell pitched against Pickens County teams and other high school representatives of West Alabama, including Brookwood, Fayette, and Holt. (He did, however, miss his sophomore baseball season in 1960, after breaking his left arm on the last day of spring training for football.)

Recalling how most of his youth teammates also played for the Green Wave, Campbell likewise remembered his sheer excitement while standing on the pitcher's mound as his team competed against "gladiator" opponents like the Tuscaloosa High School Black Bears.

"A lot of their baseball team was made up of some of the boys that played football, and they were always a powerhouse ... had a powerhouse football team," Campbell said. "And you read about them in *The Tuscaloosa News* all the time, and finally getting to play against them, you just felt like you knew who they were. But back in those days, they really had some great athletes. They had a great sports program over there. So anytime you could beat a school like that, you know, it was certainly a thrill."

Gordo resident Bobby Perrigin, 73, also remembered matchups between GHS and the Black Bears.

"We were a little ol' 2A team," said Perrigin, who played in the outfield in the minor league with the Cleveland Indians from 1962 to 1964. "We beat them like a drum. They had some good players, and it just felt great to beat a school that big because our school was so little."

—— *Red Tigers and the Crimson Tide* ——

The installation of lights on the field by his senior year, Campbell said, attracted large crowds of fans and townsfolk during games on Friday and Saturday nights. Campbell also recalled how Gordo's field was rotated so that balls were hit opposite from the horse pasture.

While most games commenced after school during the week, Campbell said the presence of a larger, cheering audience during night games provided "a little more incentive to want to show out more." Although sports failed to enthrall Campbell's mother, Mary Lee, his father, Don, often sat among the fans and congratulated his son after Campbell pitched and played outfield during games.

"He'd always tell me, 'Good game,' or something," Campbell said. "Never was critical of me. Most of the time it would be something positive that he would say."

While he played to impress his father, Campbell was also aware that others were watching him during high school games, in particular, professional baseball scouts. Campbell received a letter and a contract from the Pittsburgh Pirates organization by the time he graduated high school in May of 1962.

All that remained was the stroke of a pen. Campbell, however, instead chose to honor his parents' desire for him to pursue college. "My dad kept telling me, 'If you're good enough, then that offer's going to remain. Somebody's still going to be interested in you,'" Campbell said.

Receiving a partial athletic scholarship from Livingston State College (now the University of West Alabama), Campbell enrolled in 1963 and played for the Tigers from 1964 to 1967. According to UWA's athletic website, Campbell contributed to the Tigers' winning four consecutive Alabama Collegiate Conference championships, in addition to having pitched four no-hitters, as well as one perfect game, on the way to a 28–4 record that included his alma mater's first victory against a Division I team, when his pitching helped the Tigers triumph 7–2 against the University of Alabama. Campbell said he usually served as the "number one" starting pitcher as the Tigers took on teams like Jacksonville State, Troy, and the University of North Alabama.

One of Campbell's teammates, Bobby Fairley, played shortstop at UWA from 1965 to 1968. A retired coach who mentored student athletes at various schools, particularly Leeds High School, Fairley said playing baseball at UWA was possibly the "best time" of his life.

"Livingston is a small school, and playing there, we had some pretty good players like Jeff," said Fairley, 70, of Pell City. "[Campbell] was the number one pitcher for the team. He was outstanding. He dominated when he went out on the mound, and I don't remember us not being in the ball game and not being capable of winning when he was out there."

Besides being a "great pitcher," Campbell was a "real good hitter" as well, Fairley said.

"Usually the pitcher didn't play when they weren't pitching because they had to let their arm rest," Fairley said. "But Jeff would still bat and play in the outfield even when he wasn't pitching."

Fairley also shared his memory of the Tigers' game against the Crimson Tide, a special victory that emerged from a "special game."

"Jeff pitched that game," Fairley said. "It was a special game because we were a small school. Beating Alabama was really important to us. I don't think they were a dominant team in the SEC, but they were much more well-known than our team. I just remember Jeff went out and dominated again."

Campbell, too, recalled the excitement from competing against UA, as well as other teams. "One year we played Jacksonville State the best two out of three for the championship," Campbell said. "And I pitched the first game of the series, and we ended up losing, I think, 2-1. So we were down one game. That means we had to come back and beat them twice. So I came back, and I went on and pitched the second game, and we beat them, which tied the series at 1-1. And then in the championship series, I pitched five innings, and we ended up winning like 8-1. So I pitched all three games in the championship series."

—— *Childhood Dream Come True* ——

Campbell's dad assured him the opportunity would be there if he kept working hard. As scouts representing various teams like the Cincinnati Reds, Cleveland Indians, and New York Yankees continued to observe him throughout college, Campbell's next professional baseball opportunity came while he was going through basic training with the U.S. Army Reserve at Fort Jackson in South Carolina.

After college, he wanted to serve his country and continue pursuing his passion for baseball. Joining the Reserve appeared to be the best option for Campbell, then twenty-two, in 1967.

Nevertheless, after he reported to basic training the summer following his college graduation, Campbell said a representative with the San Francisco Giants organization received permission to visit Fort Jackson to give him the news that he had been drafted. This time Campbell happily signed, and he played in the minor leagues for the Giants from 1967 to 1973, sporting number twenty-two on his jerseys. Because of his military duties, he traveled by plane to Gordo once a month to report to his reserve unit.

Campbell said his annual contracts with the Giants progressively paid about $550 to $1,100 a month. He played in the Winter Instructional League in Phoenix, Arizona (1967 and 1973), as well as in Decatur, Illinois (1968–1969; Class A), and in Amarillo, Texas (1970–1972; Class AA). Between 1967 and 1972, Campbell threw 105 strikeouts and hit one home run, according to statistics on www.baseball-reference.com.

"Jeff was right-handed, and I was the left-handed pitcher," said Leo Mazzone, 68, of Anderson, South Carolina. "Jeff was the more mature guy from Alabama, and I was green-from-the-gills coming from West Virginia, Pennsylvania, Western Maryland, or the Tri-state area."

A former major league pitching coach for the Atlanta Braves and Baltimore Orioles who trained players like Greg Maddux, Tom Glavine, and John Smoltz, Mazzone pitched in the minors with the Giants from 1967 to 1973, as well as with the Oakland Athletics organization from 1974 to 1976.

Mazzone said he and Campbell met during spring training in 1969. He recalled how Campbell was a strong pitcher and a good hitter. He also noted how they roomed together, in addition to Gary Lavelle, another left-handed pitcher who went on to play in the majors with the Giants, Toronto Blue Jays, and the Oakland Athletics. "All three of us loved college football," Mazzone said. "Jeff, of course, loved the Crimson Tide. I loved the Fighting Irish, and Gary loved Penn State. So we used to have some arguments about that, some fun with it."

"Jeff being from the South, and me and Leo being from the North, we had some fun times," said Lavelle, 68, of Virginia Beach. "The thing I remember about Jeff was how he was a big Crimson Tide fan. He was also a great pitcher—very baseball savvy. He was also always a gentleman and never lost his composure."

While reminiscing about his time in the minor leagues, Campbell said he once hit a home run to win a game against the Burlington Bees in 1968. His favorite game, however, took place at Turnpike Stadium in Arlington, Texas, in 1971. Sitting in the dugout amid a packed stadium, while waiting to play against the Dallas-Fort Worth Spurs, Campbell watched as his childhood hero, the legendary Mickey Mantle, emerged onto the field and threw out the first pitch of the game.

"Just seeing him was bigger than life," Campbell said. "You never thought you'd have the opportunity to actually get that close to him, you know, and him being in your presence with you participating in the game. So it was, yeah, it was quite a thrill."

Sharing the field with Mantle was also special for Mazzone and Lavelle.

"Mickey Mantle was my idol," Mazzone said, "and it was a great thrill getting to see him throw out the first pitch."

"I think when you look at a great Hall of Famer, someone you've read about and watched on television for a long time, and then you get to see them in person, you get encouragement," Lavelle said. "It gave me an incentive to want to get into the major leagues."

It will soon be 50 years since Campbell first stepped onto the field as a pro baseball player. Carole Campbell, 69, who met her husband in 1969 in Decatur, Illinois, and recalled how he once hit a "grand slam," said Campbell cherishes the time he spent on the pitcher's mound.

"I think it was a great experience, and he learned a lot and met a lot of good people," she said. "It was a fun time as well, traveling and getting to see different areas of the country. I think it's something he will always remember and treasure."

It was all "a childhood dream come true" for Campbell. "I had a dream that I wanted to have a chance to play professional baseball," he said. "And I look back, I wouldn't take anything for the experience."

EMBRACING FREEDOM: WEST ALABAMIAN'S SPIRITUAL BELIEFS HELPED HER TRIUMPH OVER ADDICTION

Pickens County Herald
SEPTEMBER 2, 2015

Shar Herring can still see the burst of fire from a shotgun aimed at her face. Her ears rang from the blast that barely missed, an experience which resulted from an intense, drug-fueled argument during the span of her addiction to methamphetamine. To Herring, a Tuscaloosa resident, 37, formerly from Pickens County, meth was once as essential as a "need for air." Strengthened by her spiritual beliefs, however, she also can attest to the freedom felt by triumphing over addiction.

— "Jail Saved My Life" —

Herring often shares her mugshot when she tells others about her recovery experience. Formerly a source of shame, she feels "joy" when she looks at it now. "I feel a lot of pride," she said. "I don't feel guilt because, through my faith, I've gotten the guilt shaken off. I don't feel guilt for what I've done. If God can forgive me, then I have to forgive myself. But I feel proud of where I'm at now because of where I have been."

Herring was approximately 15 when she first tried meth. To her, meth provided an intensely "euphoric" sensation that could fill her with enough energy to power through about three to four sleepless days with little food, until her body collapsed from exhaustion.

Herring used meth between the ages of 15 and 26, and she added that she didn't actively seek it until after she lost custody of her one-year-old son in 1999. Gripped by addiction, she gave birth to a second son on January 26, 2002, and lost custody because he'd been born addicted to meth, requiring a month's treatment in NICU.

Signing custody rights over to family and hopelessly convinced that she would never get her children back, Herring delved deeper into her addiction. "It breaks my heart to see where I let my addiction take me and what I let it do to me and my children," she said, her eyes tearful. "Because it completely took being a mother away from me."

From Herring's perspective, loyalty and honesty are skewed personal values among those absorbed by substance addiction. "But it wasn't loyalty to my family members who were trying to get me to change," she explained. "It was my loyalty to whoever had the dope, and I would never rat you out. It was honesty to the people that had the drug."

Despite having facial sores, a "vicious cycle" of rapid mood swings, and a distinct awareness that she risked being arrested any time she sought meth or necessary supplies, Herring persisted to use. She manipulated, lied, and conned to continually deaden overwhelming feelings of hopelessness, low self-worth, and despair. In turn, she endured escalating disrespect, threats, and physical abuse.

Between 2003 and 2004, Herring was arrested and jailed multiple times in the counties of Pickens and Tuscaloosa, on charges of possession and manufacturing meth. Generally placed in a holding cell and bailed out, her bond was revoked after her arrest on April 4, 2004, a day that would soon represent her sobriety.

Charged with possession following a drug bust in Palmetto, Herring served 20 months of a 10-year sentence, spending 16 months in Pickens County Jail and four at Julia Tutwiler Prison. While awaiting her sentencing, she underwent rehab at Chemical Addictions Program, Inc., in Montgomery.

Behind bars, Herring continually engaged in deep self-reflection and evaluated her priorities. Receiving letters from supportive family and money from her father to buy sodas, she became fully aware of who genuinely cared for her. To those with whom she used to get high, she was "out of sight, out of mind."

As a child, Herring's grandmother bought her Bible coloring books and storybooks, memories she holds dear, but she had only been to church twice with a friend. Nevertheless, Herring explained how she sought consolation and wisdom through Christianity. As her faith intensified, she became more aware of the impact of her personal responsibility.

"The whole time I was in jail, I prayed every day: 'Lord, please take the taste from the drugs out of my mouth. Don't ever let me want it again,'" she said. "I felt like it was revealed to me that, you know, 'You can't blame this on anyone. You have to accept your part in this. You made the bad choice and the bad choices.'

"A lot of people don't want to believe it, but I'll be the first to tell you: Jail saved my life," she said.

— "I'm Going to Go Forward" —

Released on December 5, 2005, Herring abided by her probation directives and reported to Phoenix House of Tuscaloosa on December 27, having spent Christmas with her children. Required to receive supportive rehab services for at least six months, she stayed a year and a half to be absolutely certain she was well-prepared to maintain an independent, drug-free life. During this time, she worked at America's Thrift Stores in Tuscaloosa and lived in a group home.

Discharged in June 2007, Herring persisted in complying with court orders and received an early release from her probation in 2009. Continuing to work while living independently, she received custody of her youngest son on February 14, 2012. She and her older son have also constructed a stronger, loving bond.

On October 30, 2013, Herring was granted a full pardon by the Alabama Board of Pardons and Paroles. Through her constructive efforts, her self-esteem rose. Though she has not yearned for meth since leaving prison, she maintains careful boundaries with others and cautiously avoids particular areas that are associated with her former lifestyle, driving longer routes when necessary. She even monitors songs on the radio.

Highlighting the guiding influence of her spirituality, Herring also underscored the importance of self-motivation in prevailing against addiction: "You have to shake the chains and the bondage off and decide, 'This is what I'm going to do, and I'm going to go forward and not go back.'"

Clean now for eleven years, Herring's love for her children and faith fueled her motivation to change. "Everything I lost in my addiction has been restored back to me," she said. "And it's been restored greater."

ALICEVILLE WWII GLIDER PILOT'S "LONGEST DAY"

Pickens County Herald
JULY 23, 2008

"The sky's the limit."

When spoken by mentors, friends, and loved ones, the old saying can add fuel to a person's ambition as they pursue personal goals. And then there are some people who take the saying quite literally, like 85-year-old World War II combat glider pilot Gale R. Ammerman.

Raised among eight siblings on a "corn and hog" farm just five miles west of Dugger, Indiana, a small mining town in the western part of the state, Ammerman and his family helped their father, Lyman, a sharecropper who farmed for a politician and received a third of the profit share.

But a young Ammerman would always stop whatever he was doing—feeding animals, gathering eggs, milking cows—and gaze skyward each time he heard a plane fly overhead, absorbed in his yearning for a chance to someday become a pilot himself. In fact, at the age of ten, he'd already made up his mind he was going to pursue a career in the U. S. Air Force. In high school, Ammerman often made small balsa wood models of World War I planes, specifically the American SPAD (Simple Plastic Airplane Design) and the German Fokker.

133

But anytime a plane could be heard, Ammerman and his teenage chum, Bob Ring, would dart outside of class to watch it fly by. "We just loved planes," said Ammerman, who has called Aliceville, Alabama, his home for many years now. "In those days, pilots didn't fly too high a lot of times, and sometimes they'd wave at you. It was exciting."

Remaining true to his childhood ambition, Ammerman, along with Ring, enlisted in the Air Force on May 9, 1941, just four days after graduating from Union High School. They took basic training at Jefferson Barracks near St. Louis, Missouri, and then studied airplane mechanics at Chanute Air Force Base in Rantoul, Illinois, 100 miles south of Chicago.

Ammerman and Ring were practically inseparable, but eventually the two were assigned to different bases, following their becoming aircraft mechanics in early 1942. Though he couldn't recall where Ring was stationed, Ammerman said he learned that his friend went on to fly B-29 bombers during World War II, the exact aircraft the military used to drop the first atomic bomb on Hiroshima on August 6, 1945.

Ammerman, on the other hand, was sent to Maxwell Air Field in Montgomery, Alabama, where British flying cadets were trained because of German forces' domination of the skies in England at that time. For eight months, Ammerman served as a crew chief, overseeing the maintenance of a squadron of AT-6s, advanced training aircrafts that could travel at a normal cruising speed of 126 knots (145 mph) and a maximum level speed of 182 knots (210 mph) at 5,000 feet.

Although he knew the mechanics of an aircraft (airplane instruments, electrical systems, hydraulics, etc.), Ammerman said he still lacked proper training to take on the skies, as cadets were required to undergo two years of college-level schooling before they were allowed to go airborne. Because of the impending war, however, pilots were soon in dire need, and Ammerman realized his chance of a lifetime had finally come when he read a posted announcement one day at the base: "If you want to fly, the new glider program would be an opportunity."

Refusing to waste a moment hesitating, Ammerman seized his chance. "I didn't care what kind of pilot I'd be," he said, "I just wanted to fly."

— "Got the Hang of Things" —

Accepted into the glider program, Ammerman next departed to the Air Force base in Spencer, Iowa, where he first learned to fly planes equipped with small, 65-horsepower engines, like the Piper Cub, Aeronca Chief, and the Taylor Craft. "And after a while, once we got the hang of things," Ammerman said, "we'd fly up and turn the engine off before landing. We called it 'landing deadstick.' And that was our first exposure to glider-like flying."

Ammerman next advanced into the first official lesson of glider training, in which he flew a sailplane—the German Schweizer—and learned how to maneuver about and hover beneath clouds. "On a sailplane, you could hover underneath a cloud," he explained. "You can catch an updraft from a cloud and stay up indefinitely because of the plane's long wings and light body structure."

Upon completing this portion of the program, Ammerman continued his studies at the South Plains Army Flying School in Lubbock, Texas, where he learned to manage a medium-sized, or makeshift, glider. Eventually he learned to manage the CG-4A, which was the model the Allies used in battle throughout WWII.

"That glider was designed around a jeep," Ammerman said of the CG-4A. "The jeep, or vehicle, could carry four men with weapons, and when you landed the CG-4A, you could drive the jeep out of the glider. There was a cable that fastened to the back end of the jeep, and it ran over pulleys that led to the nose of the glider. So you just drove out and that cable would pull the glider's nose up."

The CG-4A was "fun to fly," Ammerman added. "But, now, flying in combat was a different story."

A month after he graduated the glider program on February 4, 1943, Ammerman was assigned to the 81st Troop Carrier Squadron of the 436th Troop Carrier Group, 9th Air Force in the European Theater of Operations. He was sent to Laurinburg-Maxton Air Base in North Carolina for about eight months to undergo mission training with his squadron. Immediately afterward, in January 1944, he and his squadron departed for Membury Air Base in England, about seventy miles west of London. About five and a half months later, all of Ammerman's training was put to task during the early morning hours of June 6, 1944, infamously recorded in history as the "Longest Day."

— *Normandy by Dusk* —

June 5, 1944. 10 p.m., British Double Summer Time. Clear skies across the English Channel.

Flying toward Normandy with a large shipment of ammunition in the cargo hold, Ammerman piloted a British Horsa glider, traveling south along the Carentan Peninsula. Although he normally flew a CG-4A during WWII, on this night Ammerman was ordered to fly a Horsa, which could carry up to 7,500 pounds of payload, or 3,000 more pounds than the American CG-4A.

Accompanied by his copilot, Billy Hart of Texas, the two reached the beaches of Normandy by dusk and, turning westward, began zeroing in on their chosen landing zone. Suddenly, a bullet punctured the Horsa's air tank, causing the craft's flaps and brakes to become inoperable.

"At some time, when we turned west, was when we were hit

in the air tank," Ammerman said. "That was the flaw in the design of the British Horsa glider: the air tank. Normally when you have flaps, they increase your angle of descent, or dive, without increasing air speed. With the flaps on, you could dive at maybe 80 miles per hour. But without the flaps, the airspeed could get up to 200 miles an hour."

Referring to battle plans, Ammerman explained, "The theory was that paratroopers would go in first and clear the landing zones of German troops. They didn't have the Germans cleared out. The Germans were firing at us and the aircraft.

"We were coming in at 400 feet, and their rifles could reach us. The main weapons that we were concerned with were the 20-caliber cannon and the five-caliber machine gun. Those were the weapons that were the most danger to us."

As a result of the punctured air tank, the Horsa approached its landing destination too fast and plowed into a thick hedgerow.

"We knew we were going to crash," Ammerman said, "so we steered—or guided—the fuselage of the glider in between the bigger trees. We still hit the smaller trees and brush, of course, and sheared off the glider's wings. But that helped slow everything down too."

The crash knocked Ammerman unconscious. When he finally awakened, Ammerman discovered Hart had sustained a broken leg.

"The first thing I heard when I came to was Billy yelling for help," Ammerman said. "He knew he was hurt and couldn't move. I managed to get him out of the glider and helped him walk about forty yards from the aircraft and hid him in the brush.

"We could hear Germans approaching. I hid myself as well, inside the hedgerow, and we stayed there till daylight. We could hear Germans inspecting inside our craft, seeing what was in the load. But it was nothing they could carry, so they just left. The medics eventually arrived later that morning, and they took Billy to a first aid station right there in Normandy. And that was the last time I saw him till we got back to England."

Fortunately, Hart was okay, Ammerman said, adding, "His leg mended well, and he flew later missions."

While Hart went with the medics, Ammerman reported to the "glider pilot collection area," where pilots who'd completed their missions to Normandy were gathered and eventually returned to base or prepped for another mission.

Ammerman said he and Hart had crashed about five miles behind enemy lines, or five miles inland from the English Channel coast of Normandy near St. Mere-Eglise, and the collection area and first aid station were located about a mile away from the crash.

Several days afterward, as soon as ground troops managed to break through enemy forces on the French coast and engage inland into France, Ammerman returned to England.

"And that was my 'longest day,'" he said.

— *Dream Fulfilled* —

After the war reached its conclusion in Europe on May 8, 1945, Ammerman returned home to Indiana on a 30-day leave and was awaiting orders to fly out to the Pacific when the war ended after the United States dropped atomic bombs on Hiroshima and Nagasaki, respectively, on August 6 and 9.

In addition to D-Day, Ammerman also flew in two later missions, specifically in Holland during the Bridge Too Far campaign in September 1944, as well as the Rhine River crossing into Wessel, Germany, in March 1945. During the latter missions, Ammerman flew a CG-4A.

From his service, Ammerman was awarded six campaign ribbons (Normandy, Southern France, Rome Arno, Northern France, Rhineland-Ardennes, and Central Europe); the Air Medal featuring two oak clusters (meaning he'd flew in three missions);

the Dutch Orange Lanyard (the highest award a military unit can receive from the Dutch government in Holland); and the Presidential Unit Citation, which Ammerman said was awarded to all who served in his squadron.

In 1994, Ammerman attended the fiftieth anniversary of D-Day in England, at Membury Air Base, where he was originally stationed. Not only was he reunited with former comrades, but he was also approached by another fond memory from his personal past.

"Back when I was training with my squadron in England, just before D-Day, we were practicing flying drills, and a kid maybe fifteen years old crawled under the base's fence and asked us to take him for a ride," Ammerman said.

"I told him, 'Boy, I'd be court martialed in a heartbeat if I do that.' But he kept persisting. He wouldn't give up; he wanted to ride. So finally I said, 'Get in there, lay down, and stay down till we get away from the air field.' And when we were airborne, I let him sit in the copilot's seat, hold the controls. Just enjoy the ride. Let him see everything.

"Anyway, while I was attending the fiftieth anniversary of D-Day in England, a man approached me and introduced himself—Tony Cox—and he said, 'You may not remember, but you gave me a ride in a glider fifty years ago.'"

According to Ammerman, Cox said he, too, was a retired pilot.

"I believe Tony became a pilot mainly because of the ride he got in the glider when he was a young boy," Ammerman said.. "To this day, I'm proud that I gave Tony that ride and reinforced his interest in flying." (Although Cox passed away in 2003, Ammerman said Cox's wife, Mary, "is still a good friend to this day.")

Ammerman has since authored two books: a nonfiction book, *An American Glider Pilot's Story*, and a volume of poetry, *Tales of Olden Times*, both of which reveal his deepest reflections on his life, military career, and experiences during WWII.

Being among those in the ever-shrinking group considered the "Greatest Generation," Ammerman feels every veteran in every branch, in every war, has a story to tell—and all should be heard.

As for his story, Ammerman's dream was fulfilled the very moment he became a pilot on February 4, 1943. For a deeper glimpse, one need only read the final three stanzas of his poem, "Silver Wings":

> But give me, please, my silver wings,
> And yes watch you how my heart sings,
> Air combat, it is a terror,
> Best not make the slightest error.
>
> Give me an airplane in the sky,
> I'll do battle up there on high.
> I'll give battle as best I can,
> And if I die, I'll die a man.
>
> They're great, the other branches, yes,
> But this one I say is the best.
> If I must know war's awful stings,
> Let me do it on silver wings.

ALL IN THE BREAK: SEIZING CUES SINCE EARLY YOUTH, GORDO POOL PLAYER REFLECTS ON PAST, LOVE FOR THE GAME

Pickens County Herald
AUGUST 24, 2016

He may have been the best pool hustler in Pickens County during the early 1980s. And yet, at the time, he needed boosts from milk crates and chairs to make shots across pool tables inside Gordo's long-gone Dixie Drive-In, once located on Old Highway 82.

Bruce Falls held a cue for the first time at age six while playing a game with his grandmother inside a bar in Circleville, Ohio. By the time he turned nine, he had developed a solid reputation as a formidable pool player in Gordo. Now a 41-year-old Gordo resident, Falls' love for the game remains strong.

"To me, pool was a way of life because that's all I ever did," he said. "Some folks went camping, some went hiking, some went vacationing—I went to the pool hall."

Decades have passed since Falls' reign over the pool tables at the Dixie Drive-In, which some refer to as Gordo's late "Dairy Queen." Nevertheless, his reputation has become embedded within small-town nostalgia among those who can still recall how older youths and adults alike would observe or challenge him in the game room.

Always eager to play, Falls never shied away from the proposition of an eight-ball competition, skillfully shepherding the numbered balls into table pockets to the dismay of his much-older opposition, who generally misjudged his abilities because of his age and small size. Afterward teasing those he defeated, Falls could prod them into trying him again.

And usually win once more.

"I saw him run the table at the Dairy Queen several times," said Tony Elmore, 54, of Gordo. "He was a good pool player." Elmore likewise recalled how a young Falls would have to lift a cue stick over his shoulder in order to shoot because of his height.

"He would play anybody," said 42-year-old Greg "Catfish" Robertson of Coker, who used to live in Gordo. "I watched Bruce play older guys and beat them. They'd get a little upset because they'd let some little ninety-five-pound guy beat them, but he was good."

Robertson likewise remarked, "I do remember a Mississippi guy who challenged him, and Bruce sent him home."

Joey Griffin, a 48-year-old Gordo resident whose mother, Geraldine, once owned the Dixie Drive-In, said, "Bruce used to be so short, and Tony [Elmore] used to hold him up by his belt loop, so he could play pool. It used to be so hilarious because this cat was so young and so little, but he wanted to shoot pool. And the older and bigger guys would help hold him up so he could make his shots. He'd point to a ball and say, 'Let me shoot this ball. Now I want to shoot that one.'

"And some people used to come by the Dairy Queen just to watch him play. They'd ask him if he wanted to play pool, and then they'd put money in the table slot, and the balls would fall out. Bruce would drag a stool or chair over to the table, and they'd tell him, 'Shoot 'em up, Bruce.'"

Falls became obsessed with playing pool at age seven. Prior to then, he tragically lost his father, Charles, and seven-year-old brother, Harold, to a house fire at their family's home within the Holman community on January 8, 1981, when he was six years old. Moving with his mother and two other brothers to Ohio, to stay with their grandmother, Falls' family returned to Alabama by 1982 and lived near Gordo's Dixie Drive-In. Frequenting the game room, he became both intrigued and inspired while watching the skills of a townsman, Albert Summerville, at the pool tables.

"I was thinking, 'Man, I'd like to be as good as him one day,'" Falls said. "So Albert worked with me a little bit. He was probably the first person to really help me with any pool, you know, showing me how to hold a stick and how to hit the cue ball correctly—just the small things. But other than that, everything I learned in pool I learned on my own. But like I said, I watched Albert play, and I just sort of got me a little inspiration to want to be better."

Playing pool served as a coping outlet for Falls following the deaths of his father and brother. Between the ages seven and sixteen, he practiced daily after school and all day on weekends at the Dixie Drive-In. At lunchtime on Sundays, he often sat on a picnic table outside the Drive-In while waiting for the owner to arrive.

"And if I was ever in the game room and there was nobody in there and I didn't have any money to put in the pool table, I would go get all four cue balls off the tables, and that was how I practiced," Falls said. "I was hitting balls regardless of whether I had money or not."

As he became known for being a fiercely talented local pool player, Falls recalled how people between Tuscaloosa and Mississippi would challenge him at the Drive-In. Amusing several and deflating the short-lived arrogance of many, Falls' wins during poolroom showdowns reinforced his local identity.

"A lot of folks kept coming in, and they'd be like, 'Man, there is no way this little ol' kid's going to beat me,'" Griffin said. "Okay. Well, crowds would get to gathering around, you know; they'd sit back and watch ... Well, when he got to wearing those folks out enough, they'd pack their sticks up and leave, and they wouldn't come back—embarrassed them."

Naturally, these embarrassments also meant Falls' pockets got bigger, and he'd share his cash winnings with his grinning mother.

Falls said the game of pool will never lose its appeal to him as an intense, one-on-one competition. "If you win, you win by yourself," he said. "If you lose, you lose by yourself. So therefore, when you win, you didn't have to rely on another man to get you there."

A LOOK BACK AT AUBIE'S FIRST YEAR AS HIS FORTY-YEAR CELEBRATION APPROACHES

Opelika-Auburn News
MARCH 11, 2018

A-Day: Saturday, May 5, 1979.

The long, blue car pulled into a parking space behind Samford Hall, its driver anticipating a long-awaited day of football at Jordan-Hare Stadium. Sporting a formal tan suit and crisp tie, the tall driver emerged from his ride. Likely amused, he turned his attention toward the green 1967 Ford Mustang parked next to him. There, a crouched student trying his best to hide from onlookers struggled desperately to put on a special getup.

His voice strong and friendly, legendary Auburn University head football coach Ralph "Shug" Jordan approached the car and asked a young Barry Mask, "Well, Aubie, you need some help, don't cha?"

"I said, 'Yes, sir,'" recalled Mask, now 58, who on that day was preparing to give his first official performance as Auburn's spirited mascot. "So he zipped me up and everything. We walked around to Langdon Hall, where they were having an alumni event that morning."

This gem of a memory recently was shared by Mask, a former state legislator. But he might be better known for having served as the first official Aubie, having emerged victorious from the two-day tryouts in early May of 1979.

The sheer realization that Auburn's beloved mascot is dancing—head wobbling—toward his fourth decade of existence has Mask and those who served after him feeling a little nostalgic and proud, knowing the spirit of Aubie remains strong in their "orange and blue" blood.

This holds especially true for Mask, now the marketing director and business development officer at River Bank & Trust in Auburn. He has witnessed Aubie's evolution firsthand since its inception and is thrilled to have watched his favorite tiger reach iconic status.

—— *Impressing the Judges* ——

A 19-year-old Mask was given exactly five minutes to suit up and make a lasting impression on judges inside Beard-Eaves-Memorial Coliseum the week of A-Day in 1979. Seeking to put on a special display to show his team spirit, Mask was well aware of the ticking clock and the effect of each passing second on the destiny he hoped would be his.

Active in plays and skits in high school, Mask certainly had experience in the spotlight. This time, however, the stakes were higher, and Mask gambled it all on a skit that featured Michael Jackson's new song, "Workin' Day and Night."

Dancing around a stew pot, the aspiring Aubie tossed in dolls symbolizing other SEC mascots and stirred the brew with a first-down marker, hitting his grand finale cue just in time by pulling out a sign that prophesied a national championship.

The antics proved to be a worthy investment for Mask—born the same year Aubie emerged from the 1959 drawings of

Birmingham Post-Herald artist Phil Neel, in the October 3 football program for Auburn's game against Hardin-Simmons.

As reality set in after his selection, Mask promptly realized the importance of a splashy debut for Aubie at football's September 15 season opener, even if it killed him. And it nearly did.

— *Embracing the Heat* —

Advised to get in "heat shape," Mask soon began building stamina for the special occasion. "At the time, I was working for the highway department that summer, living in Auburn," Mask said. "So I'd get off work and then put on a sweat suit, jog about two miles in the blazing heat. People would come by and go, 'Look at that fool in the sweat suit jogging!'"

On a hot September 15, as the mercury soared into the eighties and the Tigers were preparing to take on Kansas State, Aubie waited inside a large refrigerator box painted orange, in a corner of the end zone, an hour before kickoff. Draining a large 7-Eleven Slurpee, his breathing grew deeper by the minute as sweat stung his eyes.

"I was dying sweating," Mask recalled with a grin. "Of course, when you're nineteen and stupid, you can do stuff like that."

Time passed slowly with each agonizing drip of sweat, until cheerleaders lifted the box on cue and hauled it to the fifty-yard line. The band emerged onto the field, and at long last, the announcement came: "Now introducing a new Auburn tradition—it's Aubie the Tiger!"

"Aubie busted out of the box, did this dance routine with the band," Mask said. "And I'd already told George Godwin and Doug Smith, who were two of the cheerleaders, 'If I come off doing this slashing sign across my neck, get up under here, and get this head off. Get me out of the suit, and dump this five-gallon bucket of ice water right up under the stands.'"

Toward the end of the routine, Aubie began seeing flashes,

and his vision became blurred. The flashes turned to spots by the time his routine was over, and Aubie immediately sought relief.

"Of course, George and Doug forgot," Mask said. "They weren't paying a bit of attention. So I headed straight under the stands, and a state trooper was there. He helped me get the costume off."

A heavenly splash of water followed, and a check of the thermometer taped to Mask's chest showed a reading of 115 degrees.

"I think the water steamed when it hit me," Mask said.

— A Gator and the "Bear" —

Skeptics of the new mascot clung resolutely to their doubts: This whole Aubie thing would never work or last.

"Yeah, there was a lot of skepticism," Mask said. "This thing was still an experiment, and a lot of skepticism from just about everybody. And there really weren't any real good mascots back then."

Seeking to define Aubie's personality, Mask reached out for inspiration from the man who knew Aubie best: Neel, the *Birmingham Post-Herald* artist who had created the mascot twenty years earlier.

"He said, 'Aubie's a prankster and always up to something,'" Mask recalled. "So we kept that feature and decided he was going to be a good dancer, and also great with the kids."

After Aubie's debut, the tiger started gaining attention in the press and community. In fact, a mascot confrontation came that November when Auburn was preparing to play Florida. What started as a courtesy play fight with Florida's mascot, Albert Gator, quickly turned into a full-on tussle when the UF mascot tackled Aubie from behind.

"He hurt Aubie's back pretty bad," Mask said. "Aubie got up, grabbed his snout, swung him around a few times. The gator's head came off."

But, Aubie pulled off his best prank that season at the Iron Bowl in response to a snarky comment from Alabama coach Paul "Bear" Bryant: "If we don't beat Auburn, I'd just as soon go home and plow."

Wearing a red jacket and houndstooth hat, the mischievous Aubie appeared on the field before the game and tauntingly pushed a plow that he and his fraternity brothers had found and customized with wheels. Aubie later crept up behind Bryant, who was leaning against the goal post, his usual pre-game ritual.

"He turned around, I turned around, and we were this close," Mask said, grinning. "He looked at me, started laughing, and said, 'I like that hat, Aubie.' And I pointed at Bear Bryant's hat, and shook my head in agreement. We shook hands, but I remember being that close to him.

"He had those steely blue eyes, and I was like, 'Oh, my God. This is Bear Bryant. This is what the face of God must look like.'"

— *Reaching Out to Children* —

Children have always had a special spot in Aubie's heart throughout the years. Mask made multiple special trips to Children's Hospital in Birmingham in 1979, where he was greeted with little outstretched arms. Those moments were "really touching," Mask said, recalling how one little girl refused to release Aubie from a hug.

"It was tough, because a lot of them were really, really sick," Mask added. "But after the first time, the hospital called back and told our people how much energy they got from Aubie. We went up there three more times."

Others who have served as Aubie over the years agreed about the joy that the mascot has brought children, and confessed to how the "spirit of Aubie" still lives within them. "I still get chills," remarked Ken Cope, president of Home Instead Senior Care in

Memphis. He served as the sixth Aubie in 1984 to 1985. "During the Iron Bowl last year, when Auburn beat Alabama, I was the life of the party because I still get a little crazy even at age 54."

— Fellowship of Aubies —

Dothan resident Danny Richards, 59, who co-owns MH Yoga Health Studio with his wife, Mary Helen, served as the third Aubie from 1981 to 1982. He commented how the tiger within still comes out when two former Aubies cross paths.

"When Barry and I graduated, we both were living in Montgomery that second or third year out of school," Richards recalled. "Back then, we were out at a club, and I ran into him. He was like, 'Hey, Aubie!' And I was like, 'Hey, Aubie!' And so we started dancing and doing our thing."

When the fortieth year of Aubie tryouts are held on March 28-29, four more will be chosen to help the beloved tiger, said Corey Edwards, director of student involvement and an advisor to the Aubie mascot program. "It's an exciting time," Edwards said. "Aubie is Auburn's goodwill ambassador, and he is not just present at athletic events. He does appearances all over the country. He's traveled internationally and does a lot in the community, probably 1,300 to 1,400 appearance requests each year."

Tiger paws outstretched, Mask looks forward to meeting the new Aubies.

"We always have reunions, so you can imagine getting forty years of Aubies in a room," he said. "Gets pretty zany."

> SADIE'S HOPE: THREE
> MONTHS AFTER TRAGEDY,
> ANDREWS FAMILY EMBRACES
> HOPE IN MOURNING
> THREE-YEAR-OLD
> SADIE GRACE

Opelika-Auburn News
JANUARY 14, 2018

I pray that God, the source of hope, will fill you completely with joy and peace because you trust in Him. Then you will overflow with confident hope through the power of the Holy Spirit.
—Romans 15:13, New Living Translation

Giving plenty of warmth and comfort through its lively patterns of pink and orange elephants, the little blanket bears the turquoise-embroidered name of its pint-sized owner, a lovely name that means "God's Thoughtful Princess." At one time inseparable, the owner routinely clung to her blanket, its tags lightly brushing beneath her adorable button nose each time she drew it closer and lifted a thumb to her mouth. On October 13, 2017, she made a brave decision to part from it, a gift she received when she was born from Nonnie, her grandmother Brenda Vermillion. Having become a big sister, she deemed it fitting to give her blanket to Gran and Papa, her other grandparents, Brenda and Benny Andrews.

The very next day, three-year-old Sadie Grace Andrews became an angel. Now the blanket she held so dearly brings comfort to her family. "I do believe firmly Sadie knew," said Sadie's mother, Corrie Andrews, who noted how her daughter bagged up the blanket herself the morning before the tragedy that took her life. "Because, on earth, Sadie's security was in that blanket."

Exactly three months have passed since the Andrews' daughter drowned in a grease trap in the picnic area at Bruster's Real Ice Cream on East University Drive in Auburn. Video surveillance from the day Sadie died showed she had been playing with her siblings when she fell through the grease trap's lid.

Minutes passed before her parents and employees were able to find her. Sadie was given CPR but was pronounced dead after being rushed to East Alabama Medical Center. The incident remains under investigation.

Enduring every parent's and sibling's worst nightmare, the Andrews family has faced a crossroads of severe bitterness and a more difficult path of personal growth through suffering. Their family is choosing the latter, drawing strength each day from their spiritual beliefs and a committed reliance on hope.

—— *Precious Memories* ——

Sadie had a knack for drawing smiles from others, always rushing to meet visitors at the front door of her family's Auburn residence, all the while unleashing enthusiastic greetings to make everyone feel welcomed. She also was normally the first one to wake up, making way to her parents' room as soon as the alarm clock's light turned green to signal it was time to get out of bed. "She used to come down and come in our bedroom, and when she didn't talk quite as well, she would come down, and you'd kind of feel her looking at you," recalled Sadie's father, Tracy Andrews. "And you'd open your eyes, and she'd be right in your face, looking sideways, and say, 'Daddy, I waked up.'"

A "ball of energy and the life of the party," Sadie skipped everywhere, swinging her arms joyfully while leading the way. She was never without a song in her heart, embracing music and adoring songs like, "Jesus Loves Me," and "His Eye Is on the Sparrow." She also loved Elvis's "Hound Dog" and "(Let Me Be Your) Teddy Bear," especially when her daddy sang the tunes, a fun routine that emerged one night when Tracy wore a cardboard Burger King crown and offered to rock the children to sleep. He was, after all, the king of rock 'n roll, and he was happy to sing, using his best Elvis impression.

The routine delighted Sadie, who often made requests for a different Elvis song before her daddy could finish singing one, eventually resulting with a hybrid of lyrics. "I would do crazy stuff," Tracy said. "Instead of, 'You ain't nothing but a hound dog,' I'd say, 'You ain't nothing but a teddy bear. You ain't never caught a salmon, and you ain't no friend of mine.'"

The Andrews family cherishes these and other precious memories, including the times Sadie served as baby "Liz" while joining her siblings to play Pilgrim, a game they created. These memories preserve their loved one, forever capturing her during the happiest of moments, like when Sadie saw the mountains of Tennessee and, later, the beach in Panama City for the very first time, months and weeks before she passed.

Such memories also strengthen the Andrews as they grieve over their loved one, while embracing a resilient sense of hope. The word "hope" came to Corrie following a prayer in 2016 and has since become greater magnified in meaning and absolutely dire to her family. "I had never done this before, but I asked the Lord to give me a word for the year 2017, and that was on December 31, 2016," Corrie said. "And through Romans 15:13, the word was 'hope.' And I didn't really think a whole lot about it—I even have it up in my kitchen window—until after Sadie passed away."

— *Thankful Heart* —

A friend pointed out to her, "Corrie, do you realize God was already starting to prepare you?"

Completely enmeshed in a process of minimizing and decluttering, Corrie had taken down Sadie's toddler bed about a month prior to the tragedy. Little Sadie was upgrading to a "big girl bed," which was part of a trundle bed shared by her six-year-old sister, Piper.

"And actually the morning of, it was starting to get cool, and so I'd just boxed up her summer clothes," Corrie said. "And then that friend of mine also asked me, just shortly before Christmas, 'Did you buy any Christmas presents for her?' And knowing me—I'm very type A, and she knows me well—I typically have that done like by the summer. You know, I'm with six kids. And as I thought about it, we haven't bought anything for her. And so, again, how God orchestrated that."

The only thing Sadie wanted for "Wismas" was a double stroller she'd seen at Sam's. After she passed, her parents bought the gift.

"And that was really hard," Corrie said, tears filling her eyes. "But we took it to our church, because at that point they were asking the church if whoever wanted to give and donate toys to families in our community that cannot afford to give their children Christmas gifts. And they called it 'giving hope.'"

Coincidentally, Hope is also the name of their children's counselor, and someone anonymously sent them a book, *The One-Year Book of Hope*, by Nancy Guthrie. On December 10, the day their church was going to give its annual legacy offering to give to those in need, their pastor reoriented the topic of his sermon to hope, rather than legacy.

These instances have encouraged the Andrews, offering uplifting reference points on days when it's a struggle to get out of bed, get dressed, and focus on the things at hand in the present.

Thanksgiving was one of those days. "It's hard," Corrie said. "Especially when you're suffering, it's really hard to find things to be thankful for. Because it's easy to focus on what you've lost or what's been taken away from you, or the pain."

Though it hurts, focusing on being thankful for what they have been given has offered a helpful perspective, Corrie said. In fact, their children were already becoming well-versed about the value of this outlook, compliments of a *VeggieTales* song by Madame Blueberry and her Veggie friends, "The Thankfulness Song." The song says, "Because a thankful heart is a happy heart!"

"To be honest with you, our kids did better than we did," Corrie said, discussing how it was a struggle for their family to attend their church, Church of the Highlands, the Sunday after the tragedy. It was also a struggle to participate in their church's "Serve Days," which at the time was putting together Thanksgiving cards to accompany meals for community families in need.

While difficult, the Andrews' choosing to go resulted with more encouragement. "To see the creativity that God brought through our children at that point," Corrie said. "Sabrina, who loves to draw, drew eight pumpkins, but she put one at the top, and it was Sadie as an angel. And we don't know who got those cards, but our girls specifically—now that they're writing and they're spelling—just said, 'I love you and I'm praying for you.' And to see that from our seven-year-old and our six-year-old is huge, just to see the compassion and the heart to pray, the heart to give."

— *"Still Counting on Me"* —

The toughest times for Tracy have been when he's alone. A supervisor for UPS, Tracy said working a lot helped occupy his mind, though it was certainly still tough. It becomes even tougher while driving long distances by himself.

While Corrie is generally the more social one, it was she who felt more inclined to withdraw after the tragedy. Tracy, however, encouraged others to stop by, a reaction of which Corrie is thankful.

"Our front doors were revolving doors for the first two weeks," Tracy said, also noting how being around people, for him, has helped keep bitterness at bay. "'Hey, if you want to come by, don't call. Just come over here. Because we're going to need you.'"

"Choosing to be bitter would be easy," Tracy remarked. The fact that they have children who need them has influenced their choosing other ways to cope. If Sadie had been an only child, it would have been more difficult. "I was thinking to myself, you never think about losing one of your children, but after we lost Sadie, I'm like, 'Well, I've got five kids. And they're still counting on me and us.' So not that we can't grieve, but for them, life has to kind of be the same. I mean, you don't want them to feel like, 'Well now that Sadie's died, Mommy and Daddy are not happy so they don't spend time with us.'"

— *"Baby, She's Not Lost"* —

There are times when Corrie can't bear to look at it. As their family has driven by, the children have expressed sentiments of their own: "Bruster's is bad … We'll never go to Bruster's … If I have children, I would never go to Bruster's … Why, Mommy, why did we go to Bruster's?"

"No, Bruster's isn't bad. God is sovereign. God's in control, and He has a plan that's bigger and better than anything we can even imagine," Corrie has told them, consoling them.

"Because they're going to respond how we respond," Corrie said. "And if I respond with, 'Yeah, that place is horrible and that place is rotten,' and 'We hate this place,' then they're going to be bitter. But to say, 'Babies, no. God has our days numbered, and we don't get to choose when or how we're going to die. We can choose where we're going to go.'

"'And Sadie, she accomplished the purpose that God had for her here on earth. Even though I don't understand that, and you don't understand that, but she did what God had her to come here to do.'"

Prayer has helped console their family, bringing peace and helping to eliminate nightmares that plagued the dreams of seven-year-old Sabrina and four-year-old Cason after the tragedy. The power of prayer also banished monsters who suddenly tried to dwell in Cason's room.

In their own ways, the children are trying to understand, which has given rise to questions: "What's heaven like? Momma, why would God allow Satan to still live because he's still evil and he hurts people?"

The deeper questions have come from the eldest sibling, Sabrina, who asked her mother during the first week following the tragedy, "Mommy, do you think Sadie will grow up in heaven? Do you think that she's going to get bigger and grow older?"

Corrie thought of the writing on Sadie's casket, from Matthew 19:17: "Jesus said, ' Let the little children come to me, and do not hinder them, for to such belongs the kingdom of heaven.'"

Afterward, Sabrina remarked, "You know what, Mommy? I think God's going to turn all the old people to be like little children so they can laugh and play."

Cason, who was closer in age to Sadie and who told his mommy about how he wants to go to "God's big house" and play soccer with Sadie, recently said, "Mommy, I just wish Sadie wasn't lost."

"Because to him, he was playing with her one day," Corrie said. "So, again, to try to explain to a four-year old what has happened to his best friend. He's still working through that, but I was able to share with him, 'Baby, she's not lost. She's in heaven with Jesus, and she's having the best time. It's so beautiful there.'"

— "We Didn't Lose Sadie" —

The family slept in one room for the first week or two after Sadie passed. Since then, Sabrina and Piper have returned to the room they shared with their younger sister, and both have told their mother about how it feels like Sadie is sleeping in their beds with them.

Sometimes Sadie still joins her siblings for playtime outside, compliments of the imagination of Sabrina, who shared her favorite thing about Sadie: "That she liked to play with me." In fact, when yellow balloons were released on the day of Sadie's funeral, Sabrina had attached a note to the one she let go, which said, "I miss you. I love you. Have fun."

Once when Corrie asked the girls if they missed Sadie, Sabrina said, "Yes, I do."

Piper, however, remarked, "No. Because I know she's in heaven, and I know she's OK. I know she's not hurting. I know she's having fun."

When they feel sad and miss Sadie, the children are encouraged to pray for others, like children who lost their parents last year from the mass shooting in Texas or a child in their neighborhood who has leukemia. For the sake of themselves and their children, the Andrews are determined to continue with their daily routines. The grief their family is enduring has a mighty sting, one most would deem unbearably crushing, or at the very least heartbreaking. But it has also strengthened their love and unity, increased their prayers, and bolstered their Christian beliefs.

Hope, as reinforced by the multiple Bible verses that have continually emerged for Corrie, consoles and supplies confidence to their faith. The testing of their faith, Corrie explained, offers a purpose to their pain.

"We'll tell people, 'We didn't lose Sadie,'" Corrie said. "Because Sadie was never ours to begin with. Sadie was a gift from God."

— *"One Day at a Time"* —

Others' generosity has encouraged them, and the Andrews have met others who have lost children as well. Realizing a need for a therapeutic outlet that offers help to both parents and siblings who have lost family, the Andrews are looking into creating a nonprofit that will offer a weekend retreat for grieving families. A potential name is Sadie's Hope.

"Right now we don't know exactly how it's going to look," Tracy said. "Just sharing some of the things about our child, their child, and talking with one another about how we've dealt with it—what's helped us and what's helped them."

"Inviting them into our family, so to speak," Corrie added.

Requesting that others keep them in their prayers, Corrie said their family copes with Sadie's physical absence "one day at a time."

"Because God never promises tomorrow, and Jesus said, 'Don't worry about tomorrow, for tomorrow will bring its own worries,'" Corrie said, citing Matthew 6:33-34. "In Jesus's name, you press on."

PARK MEMORIAL TO HONOR SADIE GRACE ANDREWS

Opelika-Auburn News
FEBRUARY 28, 2018

Sadie Grace Andrews, like many children, loved to swing, especially at the playground in her Grove Hill neighborhood in Auburn. Now many moms and neighbors Sadie routinely greeted with cheer, as well as others in the community at large and beyond, have banded together to enrich the Grove Hill playground. A pavilion is in the works, with more attractions expected, to provide a comfortable place where families can gather in fellowship.

A memorial fund devoted to the three-year-old girl, who tragically lost her life last October after falling into a picnic-area grease trap at an Auburn ice cream shop, will help support the project. The process has comforted and helped strengthen the secure sense of hope embraced by the Andrews family.

"The feeling of overwhelming support is seriously as if they're being like Aaron in the Bible, who helped Moses raise his arms," said Sadie's mother, Corrie Andrews, her eyes filling with tears as she referred to the story of how Aaron helped a tired Moses keep his hands lifted for the sake of the Israelites. "So those moms are being like Aaron, holding my arms up. We can't do this alone."

"Dreaming Big"

The idea for the pavilion started with a bench. Grove Hill resident Jackie Waters—a mother, grandmother, and teacher at Parkway Baptist Preschool—questioned what she and the neighborhood could possibly do upon hearing the tragic news on October 14, 2017.

"It's just gut-wrenching," Waters said. "And the only thing you can do is pray and do anything that you think you can do to help them."

Waters said she was compelled by her Christian beliefs and compassion for children and families to take action. She posted a message on the neighborhood's Facebook page, asking if anyone would like to get a little money together for a memorial and put a bench at the playground in Sadie's honor.

"A lot of the people in the neighborhood started saying, 'Yes, Jackie, if you'll do that, I think people would respond.' And so we just decided to go get a GoFundMe page and just put it up. Basically, I said on the GoFundMe page, 'We're going to try to do a little bench. Our goal is $300.' Well, we blew through that in the first hour."

Donations of $10, $20, and $25 began emerging, Jackie said, with approximately $500 brought in that first day, courtesy of moms in the community. By the time she reached out to the Andrews—whom she'd never met—after Sadie's funeral, more than one thousand dollars was raised.

Following discussions and much prayer, the idea for a memorial bench soon expanded into a vision involving an 18-by-36-foot pavilion featuring a concrete slab to counter mud, multiple tables, rubber mulch, and shade material for playground equipment, to keep the heat from burning little legs—and, of course, more fun attractions, like monkey bars and extra swings, for those Sadie's age and older.

It is also hoped that yellow maple trees will someday line the area, a symbolic tribute to Sadie's favorite color.

"We just started dreaming big," Corrie said. "Because we serve a big God, and it's just been incredible to see how many people have come around us, just asking whatever they can do and supporting us."

— *Generosity and Volunteers* —

Approximately three thousand dollars have been raised, a result of kind hearts from the local community and beyond, Waters said. A Grove Hill bake sale on October 22, during which the Andrews children designed, colored, and sold little pillows, contributed $1,006.

Last fall, as Waters was discussing the matter with a representative of Home Depot, a man she'd never met handed her one hundred dollars from his wallet, remarking, "This is in honor of my grandchildren."

Multiple businesses—Russell Building Supply, Builders FirstSource, University Ace Hardware, Lowe's, Home Depot, and PlayTime Playground Equipment—are generously donating supplies as well, Waters said. A Grove Hill neighbor is helping manage construction, and another neighbor's relative from Knoxville, Tennessee, completed an architectural drawing of the project.

Serve Team members from the Church of the Highlands helped install ten donated posts for the pavilion Saturday, and church members plan to meet in the future to build the structure.

"It's been great for me—obviously that other people are still thinking about us and thinking about Sadie and want to just share with us in leaving some things in Sadie's memory and honor here," said Sadie's father, Tracy, who helped install the posts on Saturday. "Not just for that, but it's also for something that people in the neighborhood and the community can use."

— *"Such an Inspiration"* —

Other plans for the project will be pursued as opportunities arise through volunteers, donations, and answered prayers. In the meantime, neighborhood mothers, who are supporting the project, look forward to its completion.

Ann Garner is familiar with what it is like to face "the worst hell that a parent could ever imagine," as her 26-year-old son, Rob, passed away in 2007. Reaching out to other parents who have lost children has helped her cope, and Garner is hopeful that her actions and those of others bring comfort to the Andrews.

"There's something about having a parent who has lost reaching out and saying, 'I don't know exactly how you feel, and our children's deaths were very different, but I know the pain of burying a child,'" Garner, who also has two adults daughters, said while discussing the tragedies she and the Andrews are enduring.

Garner, whose nephew voluntarily provided the architectural drawing for the playground project, afterward remarked, "My grandchildren, who are ten and six, love going to the playground. So when I heard that that's what they're going to do in Sadie's memory, I desperately wanted to be involved."

Amanda Jones, a mother of four who met Corrie when Sadie was about nine months old, shared how her daughter, Amy, and Sadie used to ride in strollers together, holding hands and singing together as best friends as they headed to playtime at the playground.

"To be able to watch Tracy and Corrie not just handle this tragedy that they're dealing with, but to also to make it about others," Jones said, "to show love to others and show others what blessings can come of this has been such an inspiration and such an encouragement. So for us to be able to go to a playground that they are using to honor Sadie, and in Sadie's memory, is incredible."

— "Catapulted" Faith —

Anyone wishing to donate to the project can do so through the Memorial Fund for Sadie Andrews at any branch of Auburn Bank, Waters said.

Appreciative of the support their family has received, Corrie said their faith has been "catapulted." Her prayers are that the project provides an inviting atmosphere for children to play and families to learn and share about Christ's teachings.

"Especially now, I have never had such a sense of urgency to share the hope that we have in Jesus Christ," she added. "Because there is no way we could cope with something like this without knowing and having a relationship with the Lord."

ANSWERED PRAYER: SADIE GRACE ANDREWS ACT SIGNED INTO LAW

Opelika-Auburn News
APRIL 20, 2018

There is hope. With the passing of the Sadie Grace Andrews Act, there is hope that no more of Alabama's children will suffer the same tragic fate as three-year-old Sadie Grace, who drowned last October in a grease trap in the picnic area of an Auburn ice cream shop.

Signed ceremonially by Governor Kay Ivey on Thursday, the Sadie Grace Andrews Act enforces safety measures to protect children, by requiring the covers of grease traps at restaurants to be locked or otherwise secured. Unanimously clearing the state Senate and House, the act represents the achievement of a goal sought by the Andrews family, who've clung resiliently to a strong sense of hope, while vowing to do what they can to help other families.

— *"Tragedy into Triumph"* —

The Andrews family's prayers were answered inside the old House Chamber of the Alabama State Capitol building. "It's answered a prayer to ensure that other families won't have to go through tragedy as we have," said Sadie's mother, Corrie Andrews. "However, God's turning tragedy into triumph for His name and for His glory. That part is an honor. We are grateful that God's continuing to use Sadie to help prevent other families who may not have a relationship with Christ and who may not have the hope that we have in Christ from suffering a lifetime without hope."

For Sadie's father, Tracy Andrews, it feels good to have reached this final point in the legislature and "close one chapter of this book" about Sadie's legacy.

"It's an honor that it was named after her," Tracy said, referring to the new law. "If we do get some consolation, obviously, then hopefully no one else ever goes through this. We don't know why we were chosen, so to speak, but we were. And if you have to look for the good in things, even when sometimes it's difficult, I'd say this is one good thing. It's just one good thing out of many that have come out of it, or will eventually come out of it—remembering Sadie and helping others and serving others. So, in that respect, we're honored to be a part of it."

— "Bittersweet Day" —

Starting June 1, food service establishments have six months to become compliant with the law. Failure to do so will result with their being fined one hundred dollars per day until they reach compliance.

Senator Tom Whatley, who sponsored the bill, said it was nice how everyone involved worked as a team to help make the bill not only a reality, but something that will forever memorialize Sadie. "It's a bittersweet day," Whatley said. "It was great to get the law signed by the governor and for her to recognize Sadie Grace today, and the bill was named after Sadie Grace as well by Senator McClendon out of St. Clair County. This was a bill that we worked on with the family—Representative Joe Lovvorn and myself did—and we worked with business and industry to make sure that we came up with a good plan.

"It was very heartening to have business and industry who this bill would affect, who were going to have to make improvements, to come and say, 'Is this what we need to do? What can we do to make our place safer? What can we do to make sure this never happens again?'"

— "Beauty from Ashes" —

After the governor gave her signature, a scripture came to Corrie's mind, specifically Isaiah 61:3: "God is making beauty from ashes," Corrie said. "Though tragedy struck, this is one of many beautiful things that the Lord is using to further His kingdom and further safety for other children."

Sabrina Andrews, Sadie's eight-year-old sister, wore a yellow bow and ribbon in honor of her little sister's favorite color, while joining her parents at the Capitol to witness the signing of the law that bears Sadie Grace's name, which means "God's thoughtful princess."

Sabrina, who was gifted the pen Ivey used to sign the legislation, shared about how her sister always chose her favorite song, "Jesus Loves Me," during their family worship.

"I'm just glad that she's in heaven, so that she can run around and play with Jesus and all the other kids in heaven," Sabrina said.

As Sadie's memory is now preserved through the law, the Andrews family expressed their gratitude that their daughter will be remembered.

"I think that's one of the things that's been important to us," Tracy said. "Just the same as it would be I think to anybody that's had this type of situation, or similar situation. You don't want to feel like you're forgotten, or your loved one has been forgotten, and you want that memory to carry on.

"So I think with this, obviously it's not only going to carry on with us, but anytime somebody looks at this law or this bill, they'll remember the story of Sadie and picture in their mind a little girl playing and happy and joyful, which is what she was."

Corrie deemed it "an unspeakable honor," afterward expressing their family's desire to reach out and help others through their Christian faith.

"She put her mark, and through that not only will people remember her story, but prayerfully people remember how God's brought us through this, and how God has been our source of strength and our source of hope, and our source of comfort and our source of encouragement," Corrie said, afterward adding, "Out of all of this, that's my greatest desire that this tragedy would truly and genuinely forever change lives. Otherwise, it's just a sad story."

— *Sadie's Hope Ministries* —

The Andrew family is in the process of creating Sadie's Hope Ministries, which Tracy explained will someday provide a means to reach out to families who have lost children and siblings.

"Just share with them our hope in Christ," Tracy said. "Where our hope is, how we've dealt with this, what we've learned from it—what our most difficult things have been, and what has helped us the most, and at the same time we learn from each family that we minister to."

Sabrina looks forward to when she and her family will play with Sadie again.

"Sadie's days were numbered, and she had her time with us," Sabrina said. "Even though we're still sad, we'll still get to see her again in heaven."

'A VISION TO HELP': OPELIKA CHURCH RAISES FUNDS TO BUY MOTORBIKES FOR KENYA PASTORS

Opelika-Auburn News
AUGUST 26, 2018

Opelika pastor Hamlet Barnes Jr. thought he'd entered a time capsule, one that carried him as far back as the 1950s, the moment he set foot in Bungoma, Kenya.

Taking in the sights of green farmlands worked by villagers living in small homes sealed with mud, Barnes also watched as animals roamed freely, including some chickens who entered kitchens of houses lacking screen doors. Villagers fetched water from wells, relied on outhouses, and used kerosene lamps because of the lack of adequate electricity.

But it was also during Barnes's 2017 mission trip to Kenya that he observed villagers' major reliance on motorbikes to haul goods and complete tasks. Many bikes even supported three or more people as they rode from place to place. Thinking about the pastors and families of Bungoma's Seed Faith Ministries, Barnes knew what he had to do.

"I came back with a plan, a vision to help those pastors," he said. "This is what was pressed upon me. I believe God said, 'Help those pastors get motorbikes.' We can get them a motorbike to get back and forth to church and take care of the family. They can take that motorbike, and it will help them to generate funds for their families and home. Because a little bit of money is a lot to them, for the pastors to be able to take back home to their families and get sugar or buy flour to eat, or even a little oil to cook with—it means a lot to them."

— *Supporting Those with Less* —

Since around 2015, Barnes's church, Mustard Seed Faith Center Ministries, has given financial support to churches within Seed Faith Ministries in Kenya. Earlier this year, the church was able to send $1,000 to help buy a $1,200 motorbike for one of the eight pastors.

More money was sent on Friday to help get another bike. That leaves six more pastors in need, and Barnes is hopeful that hearts within the church communities in Lee County will rev up their willingness to assist in the effort.

"The Bible shows at times that the Christians who were more financially able than others, they would support those who had less, to get them on their feet," Barnes said. "Because they just need some help to get on their feet. Once they get going, then they can handle it from there, because their goal is to help others."

The pastor who received the first bike, Bernard Nato, was very grateful, said Bishop Caleb Wanjala Peter of Seed Faith Center Ministries. Peter spoke to an *Opelika-Auburn News* reporter on Monday via telephone from Kenya.

"He's so happy," Peter said. "He gets to the church better, early, and that motorbike is helping him put food on the table every day. He makes three dollars every day."

"Having access to a bike also helps him take care of his children and pay for their schooling," Peter added. "Naturally, it helps him spread the word of Christianity through the village easier as well. Where a car cannot reach, a motorbike can reach," Peter explained.

If given the opportunity, the other pastors would benefit similarly in being able to provide for their families financially, as well as attend to the spiritual needs of villagers.

Appreciative of the generosity shown by Barnes' church, Peter said the assistance they've received "is a great, great help that has changed the lives of these pastors. One was even giving up in the ministry," he added. "But through that encouragement, now he's so happy in the ministry."

—— "They Love the Lord" ——

While preaching at Seed Faith Center churches within Bungoma, Barnes was stricken by the immense faith of the villagers who have so little. "Boy, they are strong," he said. "They love the Lord; they love the Lord."

Realizing the need for continued encouragement, Barnes's church set up a GoFundMe account to help collect donations for purchasing six more motorbikes. The church is asking pastors and churches throughout Lee County to please help with the effort, and Barnes is hopeful that enough money can be raised to buy a bike each month.

"It's not that the God we serve can't bless them, but He uses us, who He's blessed to where we are, to be able to help them," Barnes said. "We've just got to do it."

"The sheer gratitude of the villagers in Bungoma is certainly memorable," Barnes said. Recalling how the pastors and their families warmly welcomed him into their homes and expressed joy during his fellowship with them, Barnes said a pastor and his wife gave him a special gift he'll never forget as he made one of his last stops.

"She presented me a live chicken that was out of their yard," he recounted with a smile. "That's a meal for them, but they were so appreciative of me being there, and they were just elated at the fact that I came there to see them and then came to their house to sit and eat with them. They just never had anybody to do that, coming from America in there to see them."

"The pastors are very appreciative of the kind hearts that are able to help with the purchasing of motorbikes," Peter said. Hoping to get the names of those who are able to assist, he further remarked that donors and their families will be remembered and prayed for every day.

"This will bring a lot of joy and the peace to these pastors," he said.

LENS ON THE PAST: HOW A HISTORIC CAMERA MADE ITS WAY FROM MOUNT RUSHMORE TO ANNISTON

The Anniston Star
JULY 2, 2017

In hindsight, the likelihood of what happened was quite unlikely. But now local photographer Dave Brandsma is a believer in the odds after an antique camera—and a special connection with the renowned photographer who used it—managed to come his way from his home state hundreds of miles away. The proof is tacked proudly to the wall of his Anniston, Alabama, business—picture perfect.

The story starts in 2014, when Brandsma received a phone call at his store, Camera Inn. The woman on the phone asked if he would be interested in buying a 1940s 4x5 Graflex Crown Graphic camera. Having trained with this model in the U.S. Army, Brandsma, 71, was very interested. After seeing it, he bought it without hesitation.

"It was in great condition, still functions and works like it's supposed to," Brandsma said. "So I bought it. I could use it now."

The camera brought a sense of nostalgia to Brandsma, but his excitement skyrocketed when the seller, Elaine Bell, returned a few days later with photos and details about how the camera was previously used by celebrated South Dakota photographer Bill Groethe.

Groethe's work is known worldwide and featured in museums like the Smithsonian Institution. His work includes images of the construction of Mount Rushmore, which was finished in 1941. His most famous photograph is of the last Native American survivors of the 1876 Battle of the Little Bighorn—Custer's Last Stand—which he took on September 2, 1948.

Brandsma is himself a native of South Dakota, particularly Sioux Falls. He came to Anniston while serving as a military photographer, and he opened his camera shop in November 1977.

Being presented with a camera originally from South Dakota felt as though a piece of home had found its way to him, Brandsma said, and the fact that Groethe previously used it was "incredible."

"What are the odds of someone bringing me a camera that was used in South Dakota?" Brandsma added.

The camera's seller, Elaine Bell, is a niece of the late Bert Bell, who owned a photography studio in Rapid City, South Dakota, Brandsma explained. Groethe worked for Bell between the 1930s and 1950s, and Elaine inherited the camera Groethe used from her uncle.

As Elaine explained the camera's background and showed him some of Groethe's photos of Mount Rushmore, Brandsma realized he'd met Groethe years prior while visiting the South Dakota landmark. At the time, Brandsma had ridden his Harley-Davidson with other bikers to Sturgis, South Dakota, to attend the annual Sturgis Motorcycle Rally. Stopping by Mount Rushmore to take in the sights, Brandsma became acquainted with Groethe.

"He was sitting up there on Mount Rushmore at the visitors' center, signing copies of his book," Brandsma said.

Astonished by what he'd learned, Brandsma contacted Groethe and returned to Rapid City in 2015 to visit him with the camera, while also riding in the seventy-fifth anniversary of the Sturgis Motorcycle Rally.

"I showed it to him and took a picture of him with it," Brandsma said. "And now he knows where it resides."

—— "Kind of a Shock" ——

Groethe, now 93 years old, was surprised to see the six-pound, leather-wrapped relic from his past. He hadn't used the camera since the early 1950s, when he bought a Linhof camera from Germany.

"It was just kind of a shock," Groethe said by phone last week. "I didn't keep track of it."

Groethe served as a photographer for 22 years for Bert Bank at Bank Studio in Rapid City. Groethe and his wife, Alice, started their own photography business 60 years ago, in 1957. Initially set up in their home's basement, the Groethes' business grew and is now called First Photo, located on Main Street in Rapid City.

Although preferences for digital pictures and retailers like Walmart and Walgreens are tough competition for smaller photography businesses, Groethe said people still want historical photos of families, and his traditional-style studio enjoys a good small part of local business.

"We still go in the darkroom and do things the old-fashioned way, like they did a hundred years ago," Groethe said. "We never quit the darkroom."

Having used numerous cameras throughout his career, Groethe said he enjoyed the handheld practicality of the Graflex Crown Graphic that now belongs to Brandsma. He last used it in 1953 to photograph Sturgis Motorcycle Rally bikers at Mount Rushmore.

"I liked that Graphic camera because I could hang over something and take a picture instead of having to set up a box camera," Groethe said.

Because of its unique history, Brandsma said the camera is

definitely not for sale. Upon first meeting Groethe, he had no idea they'd later share a special connection. "It's one thing to tell someone you've got their camera," Brandsma said. "But it's a whole other thing to take it to them and get their picture with it."

RACK 'EM UP! A GROUP OF OLD FRIENDS REUNITE OVER POOL

The Anniston Star
JUNE 25, 2017

Like a well-shot cue ball, life struck and sent them rolling in separate directions. Some two decades later, the game of pool reunited them, just as it originally united them. Now Walt Turner, Anthony Ellison, Joey Baker, and their friends routinely gather on Wednesday nights to play at Anniston's Rack & Roll Billiards & Sports Bar on Noble Street.

"Basically, pool's reconnected us," said Turner, 45, of Saks, who started hitting the cue ball around the age of four or five on his dad's pool table.

"It's a childhood obsession that we've all continued to this day," said Ellison, 46, of Oxford. "We look forward to it."

As teenagers, the friends—who also include Kevin Bryan, Scott Cheatwood, Chad Lewis, and Larry Smith—bonded through a keenly shared fascination with pool. In the '80s and '90s, they played at local hangouts like Family Funtime and Classic Cue in Saks, as well as Mike's Pool Hall in Piedmont. The latter two pool halls were previously owned by Ellison and Cheatwood, respectively.

"When we were younger, it used to be a 24-hour sport for us," said Baker, 45, of Anniston. "It was nothing to walk in during the afternoon and find somebody asleep on the table because they'd been up for two-and-a-half days playing."

"We played together at my pool hall in the late '80s and '90s," Ellison said, adding that he sold a pool table to Cheatwood when he opened his pool hall in the 1990s. "None of us had played since then until two years ago."

Pocketing balls in the side and corner pockets together for many years, the friends gradually stopped meeting, as their lives with families took priority by the mid-1990s. As their children grew and more free time was available, they re-embraced their favorite pastime in December 2014, Ellison said.

"I went to get my stereo fixed up at Walt's store, and he invited me to come down to Rack & Roll and play," Ellison said. "I went to work and asked Joey to come play. And then we invited Scott Cheatwood, Kevin Bryan, and Larry Smith."

"It was awesome," Turner said. "All of our kids are grown. From our early teens to now, it's like reuniting with a family."

"It's good seeing everybody again," said Chad Lewis, 42, of Alexandria. "We wouldn't be hanging out anywhere otherwise. You get married and have a family, and you don't get a chance to see everybody. You just get busy in life. And now, one night a week, you get to see your buddies."

Larry Smith was a teenager working a second part-time job at Family Funtime when the others were middle-schoolers playing pool. He said he enjoyed watching the others' enthusiasm as they tested their skills on the felt tables. For him, things have come full circle. "I kind of helped build Walt's interest in the game," said Smith, 53, of Weaver. "And I just thought it was kind of neat that he was the one who got me started back years later."

Kevin Bryan and Scott Cheatwood's sentiments mirrored the others'.

"It brought back a lot of fun memories," said Bryan, 43, of Oxford. "It brought us all back, hanging out together."

"I look forward every week to spending a couple of hours with my old friends," said Cheatwood, 45, of White Plains.

Six weeks after collectively grabbing their cue sticks again, the friends formed a team in 2015. They called it "Old School."

"Because we're old," Turner said. "We're old, trying to compete with the younger crowd."

The team is now part of the Anniston Pool League led by Turner, and league members test their abilities on the multiple tables at Rack & Roll.

"It's kind of like a bowling league," Turner explained. "Every player has their own individual handicap, so it makes for great competition between low-skilled players and high-skilled players. It's all good competition."

On Mondays, about 30 customers and employees from Rack & Roll and Heroes American Grille play matches of eightball and nine-ball in five teams, Turner said. About 50 players play eight- and nine-ball matches in six teams on Wednesdays, and individual players compete in nine-ball tournaments on Saturdays.

League members meet on Mondays and Wednesdays from 7 p.m. to 10:30 p.m., Ellison said, and Saturday tournaments, which are open to league members or anybody wanting to play, last from 2:30 p.m. until completion.

Through their involvement in the league, members have been able to share the same joys as Turner and his friends, including 27-year-old Scott Haynes and Katy Grace, 33, of Munford.

"I watched my daughter in gymnastics for 30 minutes, and then I came straight here," said Haynes, adding that he hadn't been home from work since 5 a.m.

Wednesday was Grace's first time playing in six or eight months, a factor she regarded as being "interesting, very interesting."

"I enjoyed it though," she said. "I almost made that nine-ball bank. That was my highlight."

While playing eight-ball with Baker, Ron Partington said he values the challenge of the game. "It's ever-changing," said

Partington, 57, of Anniston. "You're never shooting the same shot, and your opponents play differently. Some people play defensively and others play offensively."

For Turner and his friends, reuniting through pool has been a delight. They welcome the challenges that arise once the balls scatter after a powerful break. "It's you against the table against your opponent," Turner said.

Part 3

"DADDY, LISTEN! I THINK I HEAR THEM GROWING!"

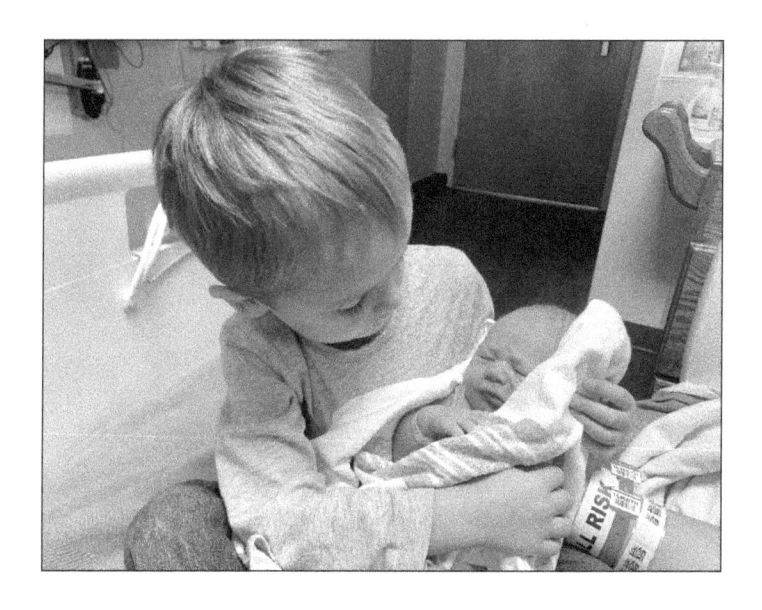

SACRED COFFEE CREED

Few things genuinely captivate the nation like a guy or gal who can drive along country roads and not spill a drop of coffee from a full mug. Pawpaw Jim Sanders mastered it, his glass cup always parked by the stick shift of his pickup. The dark liquid swayed and swirled with every bump and curve, sometimes coming real close to splashing over the brim.

But it never did, almost as if it knew better.

Occasionally, I build up the courage to put my own cup-and-driving combo to the test. But these short trips always end with stains on my seats, dash, and pride.

I am not ready.

Of course, it's not only the mess that's disheartening. There's also the fact that a perfectly good cup of coffee won't be enjoyed. That's a devastating realization to the devoted drinkers I know, all of whom blissfully embrace their caffeine addictions. And the foundation of their bliss is based on a hallowed belief that nurtures the soul and brings balance to the many complexities of life itself: Fresh coffee is sacred.

A wealth of wisdom is inherent in this proverbial outlook, which is why its sanctity must be reinforced. My retired buddy, Duke Maas, was a True Believer, and he strived to ensure that all coffee made in the breakroom was top-notch, at least from an office brew standpoint.

Anything less than stellar was presumably deemed blasphemous against the sanctity of the Sacred Coffee Creed. That's why

Duke's reputation as a shrewd connoisseur of office joe transcended the breakroom to haunt our former job's coffee supplier. The proof was indisputable after a batch in the breakroom drawer failed to score high on the Duke-ometer. This, naturally, spurred him to preach about the need for a coffee redemption, and weeks later I witnessed the restoration of order when I encountered the deliveryman in the breakroom.

Restocking our packs of java, the guy's back was to me as I approached the full pot that beckoned nearby. Suddenly and slowly, the delivery man turned to address me, his eyes and tone steady and grave. "Are you Duke Maas?"

I sensed a looming ambush if I gave an affirmative. "Nope."

The delivery man next assured me of the superb quality of this new batch, which I understood as nothing short of pure magic. Also, if there were any other concerns, everyone was urged to please reach out.

"I'll let Duke know."

The sheer intensity of this encounter reinforced what I already knew: Fresh coffee is sacred. And those who honor and defend its sanctity will continue to bring righteousness and blessings of robust satisfaction to the mugs of all devoted followers.

My late great-grandfather, Henry Sanders, would have agreed. In fact, during his time in Korea, he and his fellow soldiers endured a coffee shortage. Some relief came one morning when my grandfather spotted a boiling kettle.

"Drink this," the soldier boiling the kettle told him, and then he handed over a cup of plain hot water. But it did the trick, at least temporarily. Nevertheless, upon returning to Alabama, my grandfather made it his mission to never let a single cup of coffee go to waste—except one.

Years ago, after finishing and paying for his meal at a long-gone diner, my grandfather asked for a to-go cup for the rest of his coffee. As he started to head out the door, the cashier suddenly stopped him. "You gotta pay for that cup."

Pointing to his table, my grandfather explained that he'd ordered the coffee with his meal and already paid for it. But the cashier clarified, telling him he still had to pay for the to-go cup itself if he wanted to leave with it.

Eyeing her fixedly, my grandfather asked, "So you mean to tell me that I've already paid for the liquid, but you want me to pay for this here cup it's in?"

That's right.

Dauntless and resolute, my grandfather turned his wrist and let the coffee spill to the floor.

"You can keep your damn cup," he said, setting it matter-of-factly on the counter. Sadly, a perfectly good cup of coffee was wiped off the floor that day. But its sacrifice was necessary to emphasize another strong conviction of the Sacred Coffee Creed: You just don't try to pull a fast one on a man and his coffee.

Opelika-Auburn News
JANUARY 20, 2019

SOUSE MEAT, POSSUM, AND OTHER EXOTIC DELICACIES

A dear old friend once told me about a special dinner he treated himself to after a long day at work. It's something that always engulfs his taste buds in heavenly bliss, going all the way back to his childhood: hog head cheese and chocolate milk.

"There's nothing greater," he assured me, arms crossed and head nodding, his wrinkly face beaming with genuine delight.

Personally, I'd have preferred the chocolate milk with some cookies. But, now, don't get me wrong—I love me some good souse meat. Mild or spicy, scrumptious slices of souse loaf will always have a reserved spot on any plate of mine. It can hop aboard simply by itself or come paired with crackers and a nice chunk of hoop cheese. My appetite won't discriminate. In fact, the only memorable time I rejected any food was when Uncle Hardin offered me some boiled chitlins. One bite and the matter was settled: I am not a fan.

But I don't frown upon anyone's exotic delicacies. Lord knows I devour some unique dishes, like dipping peanut butter sandwiches in chili. This delicious combo was brought to the South by Mawmaw Sue, who was raised in Ohio, where dipping peanut butter in chili is as common as pairing peanut butter with jelly.

Growing up, I thought everyone craved peanut butter sandwiches with chili. But I've grown accustomed to the confounded reactions I usually receive when I recommend it. Like a friend of mine who once grimaced and grunted, "I don't know about all that!" This coming from a guy who enjoyed mayonnaise on pizza—to each his own.

And yet, I still can't fathom why I never see sugar cheese toast on breakfast menus. That's right—sugar cheese toast. Few things compare to sugary sweetness peppered on bubbly hot cheese on a toasted slice of bread. My great-grandfather introduced me to this wondrous treat, and I'm forever grateful. It's the perfect snack—there to celebrate the good times, and it'll console you during times of disappointment and gloom. All you have to do is chew, and it'll work its magic.

Of course, if sugary cheese doesn't strike your fancy, you can always try another exotic dish: possum. Every greasy bite will have you grinnin'.

Some of my long-gone kinfolk used to catch and keep these critters in pens, putting them on strict veggie diets until it was time for the frying pan or a steaming stew.

Bon appétit!

I've spotted my fair share of possums over the years. But the biggest one, by far, emerged one night a couple of years ago, scaring and sending our cat, Cricket, dashing inside the house.

A semi-adequate mouser, Cricket had been outside eating cat food from her bowl when what must have looked like the biggest rat she'd ever seen emerged and assumed ownership of her meal.

Hearing the ruckus outside, I opened the back door and in came Cricket, fast as lightning. She stopped to look behind her and then up at me, and I could see the genuine repentance in her fearful eyes. She would never harm another rodent.

Just keep that massive thing outside away from her, the thing I was marveling at from the doorway.

The possum continued eating, practically ignoring me as I walked over to get a better look. It must have weighed at least fifteen pounds or more. I expected it to hiss or flop on its side the closer I got. But it only glanced up at me momentarily, appearing disinterested, and then finished gobbling up the rest of the cat food before waddling back to the hole in the fence.

I named it "Walter," and that possum reappeared a couple more times before vanishing into obscurity. Perhaps something—or someone—ate him.

Who knows? Walter may have gone well with some head cheese and chocolate milk.

Opelika-Auburn News
MARCH 31, 2019

GOD GAVE US YOU

My plan was solid, flawless, perfect. Everything would go smoothly. Nothing—absolutely *nothing*—could go wrong. The whole thing was foolproof.

Jeez, was I a fool.

December 23, 2011. DePalma's Italian Café in Tuscaloosa. Evening date with the most beautiful woman in T-Town.

I'd suggested we dine out at the spot of our first date. I loved the joint's lasagna of the day, but instead I ordered the portabella mushroom ravioli. I learned that day I do not like portabella mushroom ravioli. But my chief objective was not to try a new dish—nope. Hidden somewhere within the large, multipocketed jacket I wore was an engagement ring—the ring I suddenly couldn't find.

My plan had been simple: step outside the restaurant, gaze into my date's gorgeous brown eyes while dropping to a knee, and then suavely make the ultimate move. The only move I was making, however, was a very poor attempt at nonchalantly rummaging through my jacket pockets. In fact, the intensity of my desperate rummaging escalated so fast that my date wondered if I'd finally lost my mind. Her gut instinct was spot-on.

"Are you okay?"

"Not really."

We'd reached the area where we parked by the time I finally found the integral piece. Refusing to let my perfect plan go completely haywire, I quickly devised another foolproof scheme to easily redirect my date back toward the restaurant.

Jeez, was I a fool.

"Aww, man! I think I left my phone at our table."

Naturally, my date refused to take the bait: "No, I'm pretty sure you put it in your pocket. Here, I'll call it."

"No! I'm pretty sure I left it back there!"

"Just hold on a sec, and I'll call it."

"No! Let's just hurry up and go look!" I was practically pulling her along now. "If you call, someone might see it and steal it!"

Desperate mode had completely burnt—no, *torched*—its bearings. But my stalling worked, and at long last, I popped the question.

And yet, the whole thing had so terribly rattled my nerves that I wasn't so sure I'd actually heard her answer. Moments later, as we were headed down the road in the car, I made a point to double-check.

"You did say 'yes,' didn't cha?"

I reckon she did, considering we're in our seventh year of marriage. Our journey's had lots of ups and downs, times of bliss and moments that made us hiss. But, overall, it's been great.

That's because my wife, Kim, is great—a great wife to me and a great mother to our little son.

Kaleb is a momma's boy. And I don't blame him. Because there's nothing his mommy can't do.

Need to assemble a nifty marble run toy equipped with multiple slides, windmills, funnels and a motorized elevator? Kim could arguably do it blindfolded and with both hands tied behind her back.

Got to make chocolate dinosaur-shaped treats to satisfy a hungry T-Rex? Easy peasy!

Are you a snuggle bunny in need of a companion who's brave enough to complete a gazillion death-defying dashes across the bedroom to escape scorching rivers of lava? No problem, as long as it doesn't delay bedtime.

Why, I've even watched Kim cure all sorts of boo-boos, minor to colossal, with nothing more than soft-spoken assurances and gentle kisses. And as quick as it all came—poof! The pain's all gone.

If only we could bottle and sell such miracles. Except, Kim wouldn't want to sell anything like that. If some poor kid was hurting or feeling blue, she'd simply gift them exactly what they needed without hesitation. That's the kind of heart she has—the heart that blesses Kaleb's and my life.

The love dwelling within it greets us daily through Kim's lovely eyes, the ones I gazed into when we married, the ones that have beamed with motherly joy since the moment they first gazed into Kaleb's.

"God Gave Me You." The Blake Shelton song comes to mind, the very tune Kim and I danced to as newlyweds. And now Kaleb and I both agree: fewer words ring true.

God gave us you, Kim. And we plan to keep you around and love you always.

Opelika-Auburn News
MAY 12, 2019

PAGING DR. FREUD: A GLIMPSE INTO THE MADNESS OF RAISING A PRESCHOOLER

"The ego represents what may be called reason and common sense, in contrast to the id, which contains the passions."
—Sigmund Freud, *The Ego and the Id*

"Kaleb, unlock this door. You could get hurt or break something. Hand Daddy the keys."

The headlights flashed as the engine of my wife's car roared. The stereo soon blared the "Hot Dog!" song from the *Mickey Mouse Clubhouse* soundtrack, and my ecstatic son honked the horn while rapidly turning the steering wheel.

Thirteen years shy of sixteen, Kaleb's keen obsession with vehicles has also spurred within him a distinct fascination with the idea of driving one, resulting in routine attempts at grand theft auto. Only this time, he deemed it wise to actually grab the keys. My wife, well-prepared for this certain occasion, had pulled the emergency break to prevent the likelihood of any subsequent tire-rolling. She'd advised me to do the same with my car.

I'm a Believer.

The psychology of the preschooler is certainly riddled with baffling complexities. My wife, Kim, routinely absorbs insight from child development and parenting books to help understand our son and the unique dynamics of our nurturing relationship with him.

Myself, I turn to the grand master himself: the distinguished father of psychoanalysis, Sigmund Freud. Particularly, Freud's theory involving the Id, Ego, and Superego—the three components of personality—has been helpful in my strivings to survive parenthood. While Freud referred to these three components in discussing the conscious and unconscious realms of the human mind, I view them as representing those who dwell in my family's household.

—— *The Id and the Ego* ——

Instinctive, impulsive, and always pursuing pleasure—these are the characteristics Freud attributed to the "Id," a concept that is synonymous with "Kaleb Huffman" in our home. Constantly seeking fun and getting into things, Kaleb's energy level regularly skyrockets past those of his mommy and daddy.

This leads to the next component, in which Kim and I alternate as the "Ego," as we seek to manage Kaleb's daily sprees of thrill-seeking antics. Reasonable and realistic, the Ego regulates the impulsive Id, although the Id's sheer will often proves too strong, Freud speculated.

In his classic work, *The Ego and the Id*, Freud compared the Ego and the Id, respectively, to a rider and a horse. As the rider, the Ego "has to hold in check the superior strength of the horse," Freud explained, also adding how the rider "is obliged to guide [the horse] where it wants to go; so in the same way the ego is in the habit of transforming the id's will into action as if it were its own."[1]

Kaleb is definitely a stubborn—though lovable—little colt

---

[1] Sigmund Freud and James Strachey, *The Ego and the Id* (New York: Norton, 1989), 19.

who prefers to take command of his own reins: "Weave me wone, Daddy. I do it!" Also true to Freud's analogy of a rider who's confounded by a direction-bound horse, I must admit it's reassuring to think that I'm the one who wants to give Kaleb one more helping of snacks when he's devoured plenty. I'm the one who wants to give him five more minutes to stomp and roar like a dinosaur before bedtime. "One more time, Daddy. Wast time."

—— *The Superego* ——

Lastly, Freud highlighted the "Superego," which nags the Ego throughout struggles to keep the infantile Id in check. Having integrated the values learned from parents and society, the idealistic Superego settles for nothing short of perfection. Kim and I also take turns serving in this capacity, during which one of us becomes a finger-wagging stickler in demanding that all rules be followed and due punishments strictly enforced.

But the Id rarely goes down without protest or some desperate resort for escape. Recently, Kim hauled our son to his room for a well-deserved timeout, explaining to him that he "was not acting like a happy boy." By the time Kim returned to the living room, our rambunctious Id was angrily yelling from his room, "I'm happy! I'm happy! I'm happy, Mommy!"

The Id is definitely a handful. But the impressive amount of willpower required to supervise our son is well worth the payoff in hugs, kisses, and those occasional soft remarks of "Wuv ooo."

I love our little Big Boy too. But I'd rather he lay off the sporadic road trips, at least until he's much older.

Opelika-Auburn News
JANUARY 28, 2018

UNDERSTANDING THE GROMIS, PRESCHOOLER MODEL

Does your preschooler suffer from rowdy outbursts? Do these outbursts typically occur at random (morning, day, night), especially when it's absolutely crucial that they pay attention?

Does your child also abruptly pull a 180, mysteriously becoming sluggishly devoid of all energy the very second they're told to clean up a mess they've made or told to stop fussing and get ready for a bath?

Is your child's behavior significantly reducing your sanity? Do you still have any sanity? Heck, were you even sane from the start, given that you invited an ornery preschooler into your life?

Don't fret, folks. Or stop fretting, for those of you who are too good to procrastinate. There's still hope. You see, your rambunctious little one may be experiencing a malfunctioning "Gromis," or perhaps an improper installation of such from the get-go. It's hard to tell with Gromises.

A delicate, multicolored, and immensely perplexing contraption, the Gromis can be located somewhere in a preschooler's back, or so confirms my four-year-old son, Kaleb, who's told my wife and me all about this fascinating device. Apparently, the Gromis operates like a wind-up toy, possessing a crank that sticks out of a preschooler's back. Of course, grownups cannot see the Gromis. Our eyesight is too poor, lacking the essential high magnitude of imagination that's necessary to spot this mechanism.

But Kaleb knows exactly where to find his crank. And a simple turn can make a world of difference in his ability to use his ears and make his legs work. Let me tell you.

First, however, more details are in order. For instance, you need to make sure the settings to your preschooler's Gromis are correct. There are two modes: (1) asleep and (2) awake.

Now, I suppose you're probably thinking, "Simple enough! Asleep means 'off.' Awake is 'on.'" Well, sort of. But I'm afraid it's still not that simple.

The Gromis embedded in Kaleb's back has to be set to "asleep" mode for his "listening ears" to work. Setting the Gromis on "awake" deactivates the ears.

My wife and I learned this fairly recently, right after Kim gave Kaleb a helpful reminder to pay attention to his swim instructor. Without hesitation, Kaleb explained that he couldn't listen because his Gromis was awake. During the next day's swim lessons, Kaleb responded to his mommy's same reminder with assurance that everything was alright: "It's okay, Mommy. My Gromis is asleep." Indeed, his ears and capacities to follow instructions were in fine tune that day.

Of course, it's evident when our son's Gromis is glitching or on the brink of a major breakdown. The signs can range from slothful noncompliance to hyper unruliness. Usually, with some prompting and threats of an earlier bedtime, Kaleb can fix his Gromis, or at least rig it up good, so it'll work properly for a little while.

I reckon Kaleb must get his rigging resourcefulness from Mawmaw Sue, who once used a shoestring to tie a carburetor onto a push mower, so she wouldn't have to postpone any mowing.

Rigging the Gromis is a good temporary fix, but I'm advocating for total repair. That's why it's vital that our society invest in top-notch scientific research to enhance knowledge about the Gromis: its mechanics, functions, and quirks, and of course, ways that we can troubleshoot and resolve any malfunctions.

Imagine a compliant preschooler, who declines to resist "quiet time" and happily complies with instructions to play quietly or rest in his room ... an open-minded preschooler, who's eager to try varieties of new foods and veggies ... a calm preschooler, who willingly gets a bath and goes to bed without a hint of procrastination. All of this and more is within the mighty power of the Gromis.

Naturally, as we come to understand more about the Gromis in preschoolers, we can likewise focus attention on the Gromis in adults. I know my Gromis can use a tune-up. My wife often complains that I don't listen to her, especially when she's talking about some chores that need to be done.

I'm sure she wouldn't be the least bit surprised to find that my Gromis has suffered some serious corrosion, or at the very least, is set on "awake" mode, thereby prohibiting my ears from working.

Maybe, in some cases, a Gromis on the fritz isn't so bad after all.

Opelika-Auburn News
JULY 21, 2019

HUMPTY DUMPTY: A QUEST FOR HEALING

Kaleb, my four-year-old son, caught a shark—a massive one, with sharp, scary teeth the size of you and me. The megalodon was hooked during a recent trip to Town Creek "Turtle" Park in Auburn. Browsing through a variety of sticks until deciding on one he most fancied, Kaleb proceeded to inspect a few puddles for terrifying dorsal fins, then he cast his line.

Almost instantly, he got a bite. And after a few grunts and persistent tugs, the biggest shark in the puddle was launched high into the air and onto the ground.

"I got it! I got it! It's soo big!"

It was, indeed, an amazing sight.

Shark fishing

And when he's not busy fishing in shark-infested puddles, Kaleb's other latest obsession is feeding his Hungry Hungry Hippos. In fact, very early the next morning after we bought the game, Kaleb made a serious request when he got up to go potty: "Go downstairs and check on the hippos. Make sure no one took them."

He refused to go back to his bed until assurance was given that the hippos' safety would be confirmed. I'm happy to report that nobody took the hippos.

Kaleb's obsessions fascinate me. They remind me of those I clung to when I was his age.

Humpty Dumpty was one of them. Imagine a walking, talking, blinking egg with swaying arms and legs, who wore tailored clothes and insisted on sitting atop that towering wall. We all know the Mother Goose rhyme. But it was the last part that always got to me: "All the king's horses and all the king's men couldn't put Humpty together again."

How come? How long and how hard, exactly, did they try? Were the king's horses and men even qualified to take on such a task? How did the horses even pick up the egg shells?

These were questions I posed to the adult world, in some form or another. And yet, their answers were all the same: "They just couldn't put poor Humpty back together again."

I didn't buy it. I couldn't. Here we had this egg fella, shattered and suffering, and everyone had just lost all hope in his recovery. Surely there was someone, somewhere, who specialized in reassembling egg people? Of course, the price for their services would likely be quite hefty, given the rarity in which they're needed.

Perhaps this was the same dead end encountered by all the king's horses and men. Poor Humpty probably didn't have any health insurance as well—probably couldn't get any, being an egg and all.

My obsession with Humpty Dumpty and his plight inspired Mawmaw Sue to craft a doll in ol' Humpty's likeness for me.

Taking a small round pillow and attaching limbs to it, she also stitched on a pair of shorts, as well as eyes, a nose, and a red smile. Humpty even got some stringy brown hair.

There was no need to worry about that egg breaking if he fell off some dumb ol' wall. And if he ever did come apart, he could be sewn back together. Mawmaw Sue, master engineer, would see to that.

Still, I sometimes ponder over the poor fate of the storybook Humpty Dumpty. As a mental health counselor, I help folks cope and conquer hardships as they piece together new lives for themselves. It's a blessing to be a part of the healing process, and it all starts with a person's willingness to go forward.

This could be another reason why the king's horses and men struggled to help their friend. Humpty Dumpty may have been in some serious denial, refusing to accept that he lay in pieces.

This outlook reminds me of a tree I once inspected, which had fallen in the countryside on a calm summer day. The outside of the tree looked fine, its bark appearing healthy. But the inside told a different story, having suffered from serious rot until it could no longer stand. This was revealed by the fractured areas of the trunk. That tree taught me a lot about people and the masks we all risk wearing.

No doubt, the same concern and passion that gripped me as a kid trying to analyze Humpty's tragedy still fills me to this day. You might even say that, by helping others, I'm managing to resolve my long-held desire to help my eggy friend. Or maybe I'm just being silly.

Now, if you'll excuse me, I have to help a young'un feed some hippos and fish for sharks.

Opelika-Auburn News
MARCH 17, 2019

DREAMLAND GUESTS, LINGERING QUESTIONS, AND THE DARK ROOSTER

John Lennon shared some chocolate cake with me the other night. Smiling and wearing his hip pair of oval shades, Lennon offered me a slice, politely prompting, "Dig in."

We sat across from one another, equipped with plastic forks for shoveling scrumptious bites of cake into our mouths. Somewhere in the birthday balloon–filled room, a radio played Lennon's "Give Peace a Chance."

The former Beatle swallowed his last bite. With genuine satisfaction, he remarked, "That's really good cake."

My mouth full, I concurred with a mumble, "Mmm-hmm."

We wiped our faces with blue napkins, the same color as our paper plates.

"I must be off," Lennon said. He stood and offered a hand. "Nice to meet you, friend."

We shook.

"You too, Mr. Lennon."

As he walked through the door, it suddenly dawned on me that I should have asked him whose birthday we were celebrating. And then another realization, one far more intense, sent a jolt of anxiety through me: I'd forgotten to ask Lennon for his autograph.

This overwhelming disappointment was still with me when

I awoke. How could I have let this happen? I reckon the Rolling Stones are right: "You can't always get what you want."

It wasn't the first time I'd let myself down like this. I've encountered quite a few celebrities—alive and otherwise—in dreamland. I've whistled merrily while delivering some toasted egg sandwiches to Andy Griffith, as he fished at my grandparents' lake. This, by no means, was our first encounter; I've waved to Andy at a bluegrass picking or two.

I've also sipped coffee with Audrey Hepburn, and once I even gave Morgan Freeman directions to the nearest gas station. I've also waited in line to get a book signed by Stephen King. For some unfathomable reason, I was getting the book signed for a relative who doesn't even read King, and I tried desperately to convince myself throughout the dream to get the autograph for myself.

But that's the endless dilemma I endure: I always forget to ask for an autograph. Or in some cases, when long-gone family members occasionally invade my slumbers, I fail to ask something important. Like the last time I saw Pawpaw Buck, my father's daddy, who died in 1997. In my dream, Buck was still wearing his typical attire: white shirt, bib overalls, and laced-up brown boots, the left heel giving him an extra boost to oblige the length difference of his legs. A pack of cigarettes bulged from inside his rolled-up sleeve.

Wandering aimlessly around an unfamiliar room, Buck continued his never-ending scavenger hunt for an ashtray. The dangling cigarette nearly dropped from his lips each time he grumbled, "Anybody see an ashtray? Anybody? Someone better get me one quick, or I'm gonna use the floor."

I was too distracted with helping him look around that I forgot to ask why he still looked so old after dying. I reckon smoking in the afterlife will do that to you.

Of course, there are times when some questions don't need answering. For instance, a childhood nemesis recently visited me. In that dream, my wife asked me to hurry and get an extra pair of socks for our four-year-old son, Kaleb, from the car. We'd parked in the gravel lot of a familiar country church, and right as I began to approach, my nemesis emerged from underneath the car: the dark rooster.

Vicious, relentless, extremely territorial—the evil bird always chased me and others the moment his beady, hate-spewing eyes spotted us. And slow getaways earned you a good flogging.

Blocking my path, the dark rooster raised his mighty wings and charged. But my wife had assigned my mission, and I'd rather face a flock of dark roosters than face her wrath.

I charged too.

A blizzard of feathers ensued. But I got the socks and awoke with a smile, victorious.

No questions asked.

Opelika-Auburn News
NOVEMBER 11, 2018

PECULIAR VISIONS

Face beet red and dripping sweat, Pawpaw Buck Huffman sank deeper into his recliner, his bulging blue eyes glued to the raging monstrosity that was somehow being restrained within the old TV. He dared not blink. The risk was massive—and very green.

"You watching 'The Incredible Hulk' there, Daddy?" asked my father, Doe Doe, upon entering the room. At the time, my father was a teenager in the 1980s, and his eyes instantly connected with the old man's.

"Lord, Daddy, you all right?"

Pawpaw Buck didn't answer. Instead, he called out to my father's stepmother: "Alice, if you want me to sleep in the bed with you tonight you better come get me quick… This green fella's comin' out the TV!"

I reckon the moral to that particular story is be careful what you smoke. Otherwise, you'll risk getting smashed by the Hulk, or perhaps paid a visit by some other mind-blowing entity. Of course, folks in my family are no strangers to receiving peculiar visions.

There was the time my great-grandfather, Lee Makelin Huffman, was visited by an angel. This happened in January 1952, on a day when Pawpaw Lee Make broke his arm while cutting down timber at work. Less than a week prior, his wife, Mawmaw Bessie Lee, had died from cancer.

Heading home after seeing a doctor, Pawpaw Lee Make looked

forward to getting some rest. But at some point during his slumber, he heard a door open.

In walked Mawmaw Bessie Lee, dressed in white and barefoot, seemingly oblivious to the shiver-inducing winter coldness that filled the house. The sight jolted Pawpaw Lee Make's heartbeat, and all he could think to do was gesture toward Mawmaw Bessie Lee's separate bed across from his.

"Bessie, come lay down on your bed…"

She couldn't. She told him she just wanted to see how he and the kids were doing. When she left, she did so quietly, leaving behind a serene sense of wonder.

I reckon some folks will suggest Pawpaw Lee Make's vision could have been an effect of medication he may have taken. Or maybe it was simply just a dream. Regardless, it remained dear to his heart, just like a certain dream I had featuring my maternal great-grandfather, Henry Sanders, is dear to me.

I was very close to my grandfather, who died on May 28, 2008, after a long bout with mesothelioma. That's why I was so surprised to see him about a year or so later, smiling and apparently waiting for me, as I stepped out on the balcony of his old house.

The scene was made even more surreal by the enchanting sight and sounds of multicolored wind chimes hanging at various lengths throughout the sunny sky.

During the dream, I wondered how wind chimes could just hang like that from the sky, seemingly from nothing at all except the heavens above. Likewise, upon awakening, I wondered why my dream saw fit to pair wind chimes with my grandfather.

He never collected them or anything. It left me baffled.

Still, I looked forward to telling my grandmother about my dream, anticipating a surprised and heartwarming reaction. But it was she who surprised me.

"Have you been out to your grandpa's grave lately?"

I told her I hadn't, really, since the funeral.

She then told me I ought to go by there. A relative had put a little wind chime out near his grave.

Opelika-Auburn News
AUGUST 2, 2020

REMEMBERING THE FATHER-IN-LAW I NEVER MET

Charles, Charlie, Chuck—the name and its variations are cherished in my family's household. It's the middle name my wife and I gave our son, Kaleb Charles Huffman, who at bedtime clings to his elephant lovey blanket, "Charlie." We even have a couple of spare Charlies, just in case anything unexpected should ever happen to the one, true Charlie. You can never be too cautious when it comes to loveys and peace at home.

And inside our home are many other treasured items, like photos and a folded American flag, that preserve the memory of a man called "Chuck," the original Charles—the father-in-law I never met.

A U.S. Air Force veteran, expert truck driver, and technology-obsessed computer geek, Charles Thomas O'Neill Jr. was, first and foremost, devoted to his daughter and family. The proof dwells in the fond memories belonging to my wife, Kim, who always felt secure while clasping her daddy's pinky finger as a little girl. Whether wandering around Disney World or walking down the aisles in a hardware store, Chuck's pinky was there to guide the way.

Charles "Chuck" O'Neill, the father-in-law I never met, and Kim.

— *"Just about Anything"* —

Naturally, Kim always served as the handy helper to her daddy, whom she never fails to reference as the man who could "fix or put together just about anything," like the kitchen cabinets that once nearly fell off the wall. And computers—some of Kim's happiest memories include the times she spent with Chuck as he helped assemble computers at a friend's business, which started in a basement before upgrading to a storefront.

Besides helping install software, an approximately eleven-year-old Kim would sometimes get the chance to install a motherboard. Chuck made sure his little girl was tech-savvy. But that didn't stop some customers from complaining when they peered through the storefront window and spotted a kid putting together their computer.

Of course, those folks needn't worry. Chuck could get any computer running, as well as most other things you'd find in a home. Once, he even took apart an entire dryer, fixed a vital piece, and reassembled the machine, all to the relief of his mother, who was certain she'd have to buy a new one upon seeing hers in pieces.

In fact, the only thing that stumped ol' Chuck was a frozen pipe that burst under their front yard, creating a virtual skating rink that made it hard to reach the car from the house. And the only reason he elected not to fix this problem was because he'd never invested in an excavator.

Chuck didn't take too kindly to being without a tool he desperately needed. That's why he always wanted his daughter to have what she needed. When Kim moved into her first apartment as a college student, one of her essential purchases was a little toolbox, which naturally had to go through Chuck's inspection. The thing would have gained full approval too, if only it hadn't lacked an electric drill.

— *Favorite Season* —

Other fond memories involve Chuck's favorite holiday season: Christmas! 'Tis the time for decorating, and anyone who lived remotely near the O'Neills' knew Chuck would have that house lit up and decked out.

Occasionally, he'd stray from the yuletide spirit and bellyache about the sheer volume of handmade and store-bought decorations he'd have to haul, heave, and hang to make the inside and outside of their home all merry and bright. But these maddening moments always were overshadowed by the massive anticipation for seeing the joy in his daughter's eyes as she gazed upon the annual Christmas wonderland at 217 Elder Street in Birmingham.

This same joy can still be seen every December when Kim puts out the three wooden Christmas music boxes her daddy made that resemble Santa, Rudolph, and Frosty. Turn their jolly red noses clockwise, and your ears will be gifted with cheery yuletide melodies. Those things are lucky they don't play country music, as Kim and her daddy used to ride around listening to the likes of Kenny Rogers, Trisha Yearwood, and Garth Brooks.

— *Joyful Anticipation* —

There was also Chuck's smile, Chuck's laugh, and Chuck's goodbye.

In 2009, his doctor told him and his family the sad news: he had a brain tumor. This explained the concerning changes in his behavior, like his involvement in three driving incidents on his job. Prior to that year, Chuck was always proud of his safe driving record.

In time, his tech-savviness dissolved as well. His fluency in computer lingo gave way to confusion, and this confusion spread to his understanding of things in general.

As a child, Kim used to crawl up in her daddy's lap as he sat in his recliner. On January 19, 2010, she crawled up next to him for the last time on his bed.

Chuck and his little girl shared many memories. Now they share the same joyful anticipation of the day when they'll embrace in heaven. I, too, look forward to seeing him, the father-in-law I never met.

Until that time arrives ... Happy Father's Day, Chuck.

Opelika-Auburn News
JUNE 9, 2019

FAREWELL TO GRANNY AND CHRISTMAS GREETINGS

Nan O'Neill, my son's 81-year-old great-grandmother, recently joined other family members in heaven. Granny was laid to rest on a crisp, sunny day at Elmwood Cemetery in Birmingham. She now rests next to her husband, Tom, and their 50-year-old son, Chuck. Our family expressed heartfelt farewells, and later my wife, Kim, explained to our four-year-old Kaleb that Granny had been sick. Her body, naturally with age, had become worn out.

Kaleb and his great-grandmother, Nan O'Neill.

"She needs to go to the doctor so he can fix her," Kaleb insisted.

Countering his suggestion, Kim explained that Granny's body had become too worn out for a doctor to help. She was just too sick to fix.

There was a moment of silence and then a solemn remark from a deeply solemn Kaleb: "My poop makes me sick."

He's not alone. Poop makes me sick too. But thoughts of Christmas fill me with joy, despite realizations that the season and its cash-attracting frenzy will likely have my checking account locked, yet again, in an agonizing, yuletide toehold.

Feliz Navi-*ouch*!

Ordinarily loathing the very thought of shopping, I enjoy finding gifts for loved ones this time of year, especially the kind with the potential to inspire priceless memories—for instance, the time my late great-grandfather, Henry Sanders, received firecrackers from Santa when he was a kid during the Depression. Living with his folks in the country, my grandfather smiled with glee the moment he spotted his gift. His older brother, Sam, reacted similarly while trying on his new straw hat.

These gifts were nice, but the memory of that Christmas was permanently embedded in my grandfather's mind the moment he decided to scare Sam. Throwing a lit firecracker at his brother, my grandfather intended for it to land on the ground, right behind an oblivious Sam. Instead, it landed right on the brim of Sam's new hat. What remained, alas, was not fit to wear for any occasion.

The things kids go through to get a special gift can have amusing highlights as well.

I remember a certain Christmas of my own, when Santa left me multiple notes hidden in cupboards, inside drawers, and under a couch cushion. The notes were meant to steer me to my present. But Santa must have been in a hurry because he forgot to leave one that was supposed to have been in the cabinet.

Overwhelmed with anxiety, I backtracked, reread, and re-followed the notes a million times, but they all led back to the same noteless cabinet. "I guess Santa forgot about me," I told my father when he awoke, showing him the notes.

He looked them over, laughed, and suggested I look in a certain desk drawer, one I swore I'd thoroughly searched. But there it was: the Nintendo game I'd longed for.

—— *A New Christmas Tree* ——

Barring any major clearance sales, I have no plans to buy expensive video games or explosives for my son and nephews. Meanwhile, my family enjoyed another merry tradition for manufacturing holiday memories: the picking and decorating of a new Christmas tree.

Before I got married, my family always retrieved artificial trees from dusty garages or sheds. My wife introduced me to farm-grown trees. Since then, our home has welcomed the aroma of evergreen enchantment. My father joined us last year for this selecting occasion, and we enjoyed his help once again this year.

Prior to his first marriage at age 17, my father didn't really celebrate Christmas. His daddy, my late grandfather Buck Huffman, didn't care much for it, or virtually any holiday, dismissing them all as nothing more than reasons to spend money.

The tightest of tightwads, except when it came to cigarettes and chewing tobacco, Buck saw no need for a Christmas tree. One year, however, my father and his stepmother managed to work some slack into Buck's sentiments—just a smidge, mind you.

Grabbing a pot containing a small flower plant from the kitchen table, Buck parked it on the living room floor. "Here's y'all a damn tree," Buck grumbled. "Now leave me the hell alone!"

Ecstatic, my father and his stepmother got some decorations for the flower and hung pretty lights and tinsel on it—and presto! Christmas magic, merry and bright, filled the Buck Huffman household—at least until Buck got antsy over the light bill.

My father shared this memory as we perused the many rows of trees. Pointing to some of the bigger ones, I asked him how they compared with his Christmas flower. Eyeballing a price tag attached to a branch the color of money, my father offered a fair estimate.

"Daddy's was cheaper."

My wallet agreed. But, Lord Almighty, what a tree! And we took it home to decorate, joyfully.

Opelika-Auburn News
DECEMBER 9, 2018

MERRY CHRISTMAS, SANTA

"Ho-ho-ho!" wheezed the jolly, tall Saint Nick, his trim and lanky physique at odds with the lumpy pillow that filled his coat and drooped awkwardly from over his belt. Santa's belly looked more bloated than merrily plump, but that didn't stop families from greeting him with cheer the moment he entered their homes to deliver a special gift to a special kid in need.

Mr. Claus' sleigh that year was a maroon 1980s Ford pickup, a stylish gas-guzzler driven by a sarcastic elf, who kept the stereo tuned to Southern rock. It was Christmas morning, an early one, and the yuletide duo dashed through town to deliver two gifts with glee: one for a little boy and the other for a precious girl. Both children were ecstatic to see the merry gift bearer, who mirrored their enthusiasm. Santa even obliged the families and children who swarmed around him when his sleigh made its last stop at an apartment complex.

"Oh, Lawd," the elf muttered upon seeing the families charge. But Santa welcomed them all, radiating enchantment while posing for pictures and chatting with all the happy tots.

The scene tickled the elf, whose heart swelled with joy. The elf could remember how, when he was an elfin child, his Christmas once came in a little box. His family didn't have much, and he'll never forget the football and candy that were delivered to his door by others whose hearts brimmed with care. They also brought the elf's sister a dolly, the additional sugary sweets complementing her and her sweet smiles.

Indeed, the elf felt good knowing he'd helped spread some holiday cheer. It was this very feeling of delight that inspired his desire to get gifts for children who otherwise wouldn't open any on Christmas, usually leaving them outside front doors late on Christmas Eve.

And Santa? This particular Kris Kringle has always enjoyed helping others. In elementary school, he used to assist a dear friend who used a wheelchair to get around. Santa routinely opened doors and made sure his grateful comrade reached the bus to go home.

A rambling wisecracker who regularly speaks volumes about absolutely nothing, Santa took his gabbiness to a new level when he learned sign language. In fact, his fluency amazed the elf one day while they hunted deer. As Santa demonstrated his mastery, a doe wandered near and, eventually, away from the shooting house. Another elf, who watched the same deer from afar, wondered frantically why no shots were being fired.

It wasn't the last time this Santa's actions, intentional or not, spurred panic and frustration among those who cherish him. For a time, years after he and the elf delivered gifts, Santa lived the hard life on the streets, toting his few belongings in a duffel bag wherever he roamed.

The times Santa landed in jail were a huge relief to the elf, who reasoned that as long as Santa was there, Mr. Claus was guaranteed a roof and three meals daily. Each week, the elf put some money on Santa's books to help him out a little—that, plus many, many prayers.

Soon those prayers were answered, as Santa got a much more serious grip on the reins of his life and gradually managed to get things together. Now the twinkle, once faded from his eyes, has returned. It beams triumphantly.

Life can be rough, Santa will tell you. But there are a lot of things in this world to appreciate, like family, a good meal, and a warm home.

Santa has since earned his GED, gotten a good job, and paid off all his fines. If all goes well, and those who've always believed in him somehow make it on his "nice" list, maybe he'll call or pay us a little visit this year. After all, it simply wouldn't be Christmas without Santa Claus.

Opelika-Auburn News
DECEMBER 16, 2018

ENOUGH FUN TO FILL A BILLFOLD

Please don't tell him, but I'm giving my four-year-old son the little billfold I was given when I was his age. Featuring an engraved image of a trophy buck standing next to a doe drinking from a stream, the leather billfold used to fill my back pocket every time I went to town and, later, school.

Occasionally, if I forgot to bring a toy for show and tell, I'd happily whip out my billfold and explain why it was so special to me: "When I'm the richest man in the world, I'm gonna keep all my money in here."

Sometimes there'd be a dollar or two inside, to emphasize my point, the bills always folded or hastily wadded so they'd fit. The wallet's length was slightly shorter than an uncrumpled dollar.

The riches I envisioned have yet to come, at least from a financial standpoint. But I'm truly blessed with other riches; I'm wealthy with the love of a family and happy experiences that will always warm my heart. Many of these experiences involve my son, Kaleb, who never fails to inspire smiles. For instance, it's Kaleb who often reminds me to hug my finger. You should probably hug yours if you haven't been doing so. Fingers have feelings too.

Kaleb has also taught me that, apparently, some little boys operate off of imaginary gasoline, or at least our model does. Sometimes, when he's running full blast, riding his bike, or absorbed in engineering the layout of toy train tracks, Kaleb will suddenly come to a full halt. "I need more gas, Daddy," he says.

Grabbing a can from my imaginary supply, which I keep stocked at all times, I then remove the fuel cap from his back and give him a full refill. Instantly the gears, sprockets, and various other mechanisms resume their functions, and Kaleb is at it again. "Thank you, Daddy," he says.

I'd much rather hear those words than abruptly be informed that my invitation to Kaleb's next birthday party has been withdrawn. Word of this unanimous 1–0 vote usually comes when Kaleb faces consequences after misbehaving. "You're not coming to my birthday, Daddy!" he says.

It's going to be a little hard to help put together a birthday party that I'm not allowed to attend next September. But I reckon I'll figure something out.

At least I didn't eat Kaleb's dinosaur, the one he dreamed about recently. My wife, Kim, is guilty of that misdeed, having trespassed into our son's dream. Or at least that's how we've all come to understand it. And the scornful reminders of her offense are intense enough to cause even the most devout carnivores to become flooded with shame.

"I'm mad at you, Mommy. You ate my dinosaur."

"Baby, I didn't eat your dinosaur," Kim said. But Kaleb doesn't let her off that easy. Conducting shrewd, gut-wrenching prosecutions is an art he's mastered.

"Yes. You. Did. You ate my dinosaur. You don't do that."

The wound is deep. Its scar, should it ever be allowed to scab over and heal, will undoubtedly be a tragic reference in family discussions for generations. You just don't go in someone's dream and eat their dinosaur.

Solace for this offense, nevertheless, can be found through the joy felt while playing "Monster." A bedtime ritual, this game requires two terrified humans to run from a roaring monster and hide under a predetermined blanket.

All three of us get a turn at playing the spine-chilling creature of doom, which once evolved into a "bunny monster," after Kaleb's preschool got a pet rabbit. You'll know when the bunny monster is coming because its giant hind feet stomp and walk like a sumo wrestler.

Playing the monster requires Broadway-worthy acting skills. Half-hearted roars, mediocre monstrous intensity while tracking humans, and failures to reach the blanket within an expected timeframe always result in do-overs.

Kaleb demands perfection.

I don't blame him. His expectations have helped craft many fun experiences, and I'm grateful for the ones we've shared so far. There's more than enough of them to fill the little billfold I'm giving him.

We're rich.

Opelika-Auburn News
DECEMBER 23, 2018

"THE AVON MAN" AND OTHER GIFT-GIVING EXPLOITS

Ding-dong! Avon calling.

And, sure enough, Pawpaw Buck Huffman answered. His leather saddlebags packed with bookoos of cosmetics—sparkling lipstick, exotic perfumes, glamorous nail polish, mascara, etc.—the old man straddled his motorcycle and roared into town, all set to deliver the goods. And everywhere he stopped, he was greeted with cheer by housewives and bachelorettes eager to get their orders, all of them aiming to keep or attract a mate.

Naturally, Pawpaw Buck understood their game plan perfectly, as he himself was striving to keep a lady friend happy. She was a pro at selling Avon products, so much so that she needed help delivering all the door-to-door and beauty shop orders she collected, especially during the Christmas season.

Never fear—Pawpaw Buck was near. And that's how he became the "Avon Man."

It was a role he pulled off beautifully.

Memories like these tend to bubble up around this time of year, when I'm out here hustling and trying to find the perfect gift for my wife—to keep her happy. My son, Kaleb, has one-upped me, having already given his mommy an early Christmas gift. He had to give it early. Wrapping a pretty bouquet of Christmas flowers is virtually impossible — if you want to keep the flowers alive.

Of course, there's nothing wrong with giving an early present. This way, I know exactly how high the gift-giving bar's been set: sky-high.

And yet, there's quite a bit of wiggle room when it comes to giving "meaningful" gifts. Sometimes simply doing a good deed will do. That way you don't have to worry about tasking your ignorant hands with any wrapping jobs or making sure an ornery bow stays stuck on a present.

Good deeds—I reckon the Avon Man was on to something. It sure beats what my father used to do: break up with girlfriends right before big holidays or birthdays. You could always make up afterward—maybe.

Of course, that cop-out is a lot harder to pull off when you've tied the knot. The risk is ill-advised. I figured I better play it safe and get my wife a gag gift, like the whoopee cushion my great-grandfather, Henry Sanders, once got for a coworker. Expecting a laugh and perhaps an incredulous gesture after the present was opened, my grandfather instead found himself looking into a pair of misty eyes as the coworker's face radiated the most genuine sense of sincere appreciation. The guy told my grandfather it would probably be the only thing he'd get that Christmas. My grandfather, in turn, wished he'd given something better.

Sometimes it's a total crapshoot when it comes to knowing whether a gift's going to be cherished or tossed into junk-drawer oblivion. I wouldn't be a bit surprised if many of my gifts are buried under decades-old catalogues, long-lost ink pens, random rubber bands, and discarded love letters from cackling debt collectors.

Still, I hope some of my gifts managed to get put away somewhere better, perhaps even taken out occasionally for an admiring look. I'm referring to the ones I worked my tail off to buy, like the fancy Kmart jewelry I bought for a girlfriend back in middle school. Earning enough money required lots of firewood to be split, brush to be cleared, feed to be hauled, and horse stalls to be shoveled.

There were six stalls in Pawpaw Jim's barn, one of which measured about the length of three. It was reserved for a mare and her colt. Always looking to seal a good deal, Pawpaw Jim offered to pay me five dollars per shoveled stall. Without hesitation, I agreed. But it was this very lack of hesitation that caused me to earn only five dollars for the extra-long stall. Business negotiating was not my strong suit.

And so I shoveled and shoveled, repeatedly filling a wheelbarrow and dumping it outside the barn. Hoping to get fed, the horses hung out for a while and watched intently, their disgruntled neighing indicating their frustration over empty troughs. At some point they left, though some took it upon themselves to spite me by adding to my workload.

Eventually, I earned enough money to buy my perfect Kmart gift, and I was excited to give it to my girlfriend before school closed for Christmas break. In turn, she gave me two movies: *Independence Day* and *Python*. To this day I'm still haunted by a nagging suspicion that those movies came from a bargain bin. But I was extremely grateful all the same.

Now I'm getting the perfect gift for my wife. She never asks for much, but she deserves the very best—within a reasonable price range. Otherwise, I'd have to find some quick side work.

Perhaps I could give Avon a try. It's a Huffman tradition, after all.

Opelika-Auburn News
DECEMBER 22, 2019

COUNTRY PETS: COW, RACCOON, GATOR

She should've been born a dog. Alas, fate chose otherwise, and she emerged a cow—but, golly, what a happy cow, perhaps the happiest in the world.

I remember well the moment I gained her acquaintance, many years ago during my childhood. Visiting family in Ohio, I'd tagged along with my much-older cousin, who babbled endlessly about his expertise in shooting unwanted varmints while giving me a tour of their farm and showing me all the animals. Chickens, pigs, ducks—finally, we got to the cattle. And instantly, a rambunctious heifer came galloping toward us, full steam, leaping merrily into the air about midway in her approach.

Sticking her head over the fence, she unleashed a rejoiceful, "Moo!" and then a massive glob of tongue hung from a corner of her magnificent smile.

"You can pet her," my cousin told me. "She don't bite. She'll lick ya to death, though."

He was right. And anytime we were outside, that cow followed alongside us the best she could on the other side of the fence, galloping, leaping, and mooing, tongue hanging out the corner of her smile. The minute we stopped, she'd stretch her head over the fence and gesture for a gentle pat or scratch on the noggin. Occasionally, my cousin treated her to a cigarette or two, which she scarfed down with jaw-smacking gusto.

It was, at the time, the most amazing thing I'd ever seen. I wished I could take her home to Alabama. I'd have named her "Rufus" and hugged her each time I stepped off the school bus by the mailbox, right where she and my dogs would be sitting and waiting for me.

If she'd been born a dog, she could have been the best pet I ever had ... just like the special pet that belonged to my wife's uncle, Rick, in the 1960s.

— *A Raccoon and Her Human* —

"Matilda" was her name. And she was the best raccoon pal a tenth grader could have ever welcomed into his life.

A dogfood fanatic, Matilda—like Rufus the cow—enjoyed a good cigarette as well. Her tobacco obsession began shortly after she was discovered as a baby in the woods just outside of Jasper.

The proof was evident by the teeny punctures that once riddled a visiting relative's cigarette. "What in the world?" Aunt Billie remarked after taking her cig out of her bag, spinning it between her fingers to observe all the mysterious marks. This was only a mere taste of the much bigger shenanigans that inevitably followed, as Matilda grew to become a compulsive tobacco hoarder.

This didn't bode well for Rick's parents, who always kept at least ten to twelve cartons of Winstons in their pantry. Naturally, ol' Matilda got a good whiff of this, and she thought it fitting to shred all the cigarettes and pile the huge mass of tobacco in the corner of a cabinet—for safe keepin'.

Yessiree, Matilda was full of surprises, and she got along well with the family dogs. Spending a lot of time with a Labrador called "Fitch," Matilda used to bite fleas off her good friend. Grateful, Fitch returned the favor.

Once, after a litter of puppies debuted under Rick's childhood home, Matilda made it her business to keep the momma dog company. Perhaps she even puppy-sat on occasion.

It was also around this time that the gas heater needed repairing, and a repairman had to crawl under the house to do his job. Almost instantly, he was ambushed by several rowdy puppies, as well as an equally rambunctious Matilda, who took a seat on the man's head and nibbled on his ears

Of course, Matilda's favorite sitting spot was atop Rick's shoulders. The two shared a practically inseparable bond, so much so that Matilda even had her own special way of communicating with her human companion. At night, or whenever she deemed it time to come inside, this witty raccoon would crawl under the house and up into the floor furnace and then head toward the grate in Rick's bedroom. Hanging onto the floor grate with one paw, Matilda would rake it with her other, until Rick awoke to lift the grate and let her in.

There was never a dull moment with Matilda. That's why Rick was heartbroken when she suddenly disappeared. He searched everywhere for her, but there was no sign of his beloved ring-tailed pal.

All seemed lost, until his teacher, who lived about two miles down the road from Rick, asked if his missing raccoon liked dogfood. Matilda was, indeed, a dogfood fanatic. And she was, indeed, the very critter that kept seizing the stash on the teacher's back porch. Seeing Rick, she wasted no time leaping back onto his shoulder.

The only thing Matilda liked more than dogfood was her human. And she stayed with Rick until the "call of the wild" phoned and beckoned her away.

— *The Watchful "Pedro"* —

It was a shame Matilda didn't stick around as long as Pedro the alligator, who once dwelled in Rick's family's pond. Pedro initially belonged to a family friend, who brought the gator as a baby to Alabama from Florida, to live in a minnow pond.

Rick's father, nevertheless, gained custody after Pedro gave the friend a good scare by snapping its jaws behind him while he was busy pulling up a minnow-full net. The friend aimed to kill the gator, who by then was about four feet long. But Rick's father assured him he'd take the thing off his hands. He even had a bigger pond to put it in, and that's where Pedro lived for about six years, reaching a good eight feet in length.

Always watchful, the gator's eyes poked up out of the water as Rick and his siblings played on the shore nearby. Pedro did similarly when he was fed meat scraps, routinely alerted to supper time when Rick's father slapped the water with a wood board.

Pedro, unfortunately, met his demise after wandering out of the pond and into a nearby field, where a neighbor was busy bush hoggin'. To honor his memory, the gator was stuffed and mounted on the wall over a china cabinet.

Perhaps ol' Pedro would've been better off if he'd been born a dog, or a raccoon.

Opelika-Auburn News
AUGUST 18, 2019

CATS: THEY'RE GOOD PEOPLE

> Time spent with cats is never wasted.
> —Sigmund Freud

"Cod" was what he went by, Ol' Big Cod. And anytime his name came up at the old feed mill in my hometown, folks knew things were about to get serious.

That's because Cod took his work seriously, very serious. And he earned everything he had, especially his good job that kept his big belly full and gave him top-notch health care.

Yessiree, Ol' Cod cat-apulted his way to the top, and all he had to do to stay up there was keep making sure all unwanted critters abided by the mill's "no trespassing" policy. Ask any reformed rodent, raccoon, or humbled street mutt, and they'll agree: there was no escaping Cod's deadly judo swipe.

He was one mean kung fu fightin' kitty.

In fact, Cod made such a big impression that the mill workers who adopted him and made sure he got to his vet appointments did something special: Cod was awarded "employee of the year." The framed picture in the break room said so. Ol' Cod's gone now, but his whiskered legacy lives on.

The same goes for the cats who curled their ways up into my life. Take Lucky, for instance, a striped gray tomcat who earned his name for one good reason, particularly because of all the rough dogs that roamed my childhood neighborhood. Lucky was *lucky* he stayed alive.

He held his own, though, and he hung around for a long time, even once returning home after riding for miles to school under the hood of our pickup. No one realized he was under there until he shot out and vanished down the road.

We figured that was the last we'd see of him. But ol' Lucky greeted us under the carport about a week later, eager to keep catching rats from our backyard shed and delivering his kills to the front door mat. All of them would be arranged in a neat row, meticulously spaced apart, like trophies on display.

My mother wasn't a fan of Lucky's deliveries. She told him so and then asked if he'd kindly start taking his kills elsewhere. Lucky settled for her flower bed.

Another great feline was good ol' Jersey, a paunchy black cat who lived his life under the delusion that he was a dog. In fact, I wouldn't be a bit surprised if Jersey held a prestigious rank—or at least an honorary one—within the American Canine Association.

Sure, some may say Jersey thought he was applying for membership in the other ACA, the American Cat Association. But those who truly knew him knew better. No "true" cat would have allowed himself to be dressed up as a jolly elf every Christmas and never seek vengeance.

Jersey had the earthly body of a cat but the soul of a purebred Labrador. Extremely outgoing, playful, and loyal, Jersey also was a skilled duck hunter, as evidenced by all the feathers that had to be plucked from his fur upon his triumphant returns from a nearby pond.

Jersey would have made a fine bird dog—sort of. Once he managed to haul a huge one into the house through his cat door in the window. Only he failed to put the poor thing out of commission, resulting with it flapping wildly around the bedroom and showering feathers everywhere. My wife, Kim, nearly died.

Of course, Kim was the one who adopted Jersey, having discovered him at the Humane Society's "Cat House" in Tuscaloosa. From the time she stepped inside to look at all the prospective furry pals, Kim found herself being pursued by ol' Jersey, who meowed nonstop and stayed under her until she finally decided to just carry him around. By the end of her visit, Kim reckoned she'd take home the cat that refused to be put down.

Naturally, this evolved into Kim toting Jersey around the house in a baby carrier wrap to keep him content. And then it evolved again, years later, when our son, Kaleb, started lugging Jersey around like a sack of potatoes. That cat loved Kaleb, but it was obvious he much preferred the baby wrap.

Jersey departed this world last year, passing from old age. His final week was his cuddliest.

Now two black kittens have taken his place. It took two to fill the mighty void Jersey left behind. One of them, whose chest and feet are white, goes by "Oreo." He's convinced he's a dog too, always licking and slurping on whoever's nearby. The other kitten, Shadow, likes to eat plastic bags and wrappers.

Never a dull moment with cats—they're good people.

Opelika-Auburn News
FEBRUARY 2, 2020

HOME IS WHERE THE BIRDS ARE

NEST FOR RENT.

Somewhere atop my hanging porch light, I reckon I'll need to post a little sign that says this. Can't do it now, though.

No vacancy.

A soon-to-be-mama bird is our newest guest, having settled into the state-of-the-art nest that welcomed my family on our front porch when we moved into our house a few years ago. I'm sure this bird plans to stay as long as the last one.

Now, I'm not exactly sure how long a mama bird's maternity leave is supposed to be. But it sure didn't take our last renter long to hatch her babies, feed those winged munchkins and launch 'em all out into the world.

Birds don't waste time.

Finding another renter, however, took forever. Two summers ago was the last time the nest was occupied, although a neighbor told me it normally got used every summer.

If those previous guests were anything like the last one we had, they bailed when rent came due.

Now, our newest renter is a lot louder and much more cautious than the last one. She dive-bombs our cat, Shadow, every time he steps outside. Likewise, another bird, whom I assume is either the daddy or a hired bodyguard, routinely joins the mama in a tag-teaming frenzy against Shadow, unleashing squawks of warfare while zeroing in on their whiskered target.

Initially, Shadow seemed amused by these front-yard ambushes. Now he just looks annoyed, occasionally looking up at me with yellow eyes that seem to say, "Seriously... How much longer 'til these pesky things pack up and leave?"

Shadow is strongly pushing for us to look into revising our eviction policy.

In the meantime, I'm looking forward to seeing the new hatchlings. The last batch literally burst out of the nest when they took off, like a shook-up bottle of soda. They probably would've stayed longer in that nest if there'd been any room left.

One thing's for sure, whoever built the nest knew what they were doing. Sturdy and weatherproof, the thing consists of layers of thick mud, twigs, grass and pine straw.

A drapery of moss decorates the exterior.

It's amazing what can be used to make or maintain a home. In fact, many decades ago while strolling through the countryside, my great-grandfather, Henry Sanders, once stumbled upon the peculiar sight of an old timer going 'round and round an old shack with a roll of plastic wrap.

The old timer had made good progress wrapping his home, and my grandfather simply had to ask, "Hey! What're you doing there?"

Without stopping, the old man called out a single word.

"Insulation."

Use what you got, friends. But I reckon the best part of any home—at least for me—is the people you share it with, including the neighbors.

My great-aunt, Betty Jean, will agree.

Many years ago during the mid-1940s, her daddy, Pawpaw Lee Makelin Huffman, broke his back in three or four places after a tree fell on him while he was at work cutting down timber.

Rushed to a hospital in Birmingham, Pawpaw Lee Make stayed there for a long time. Aunt Betty Jean, who was about five or six at the time, cried because she thought her daddy was never coming home. But in the midst of tragedy, generosity shone through.

The neighbors came over and planted Pawpaw Lee Make's crop.

Afterward, to Aunt Betty Jean's surprise and relief, her daddy finally came home and wasted no time gathering the crop. Everyone, including the neighbors, was glad to welcome him back.

After all, birds of a feather …

Opelika-Auburn News
JUNE 7, 2020

HE'S STILL A GIANT

Even now, at his smallest, he's still a giant.

The last few weeks were mighty rough on Pawpaw Jim Sanders. Hospitalized and receiving treatment for pneumonia, during which 1.7 liters of fluid were drained off his lungs, he also underwent a heart cath procedure.

The test revealed that, at some point, Pawpaw Jim had suffered a heart attack, and now he needs double bypass surgery. This can be done after multiple blood clots are dissolved, especially a big one in his lungs.

The next day, after receiving all the news about his heart, Pawpaw Jim was told he has kidney cancer. His doctor assured him it's treatable.

That word—"treatable"—brought some brightness back to his pale face. But he was absolutely beaming when the doctor finally discharged him.

His eagerness to get back home was matched by that of family and friends, who'd been praying for his return. We're glad he's back in his recliner.

Still, he's got a long, tough road ahead of him.

This realization really sank in as I looked down at Pawpaw Jim as he lay on his bed. Now, I'd visited him in the hospital, but somehow it was different seeing him resting, semi-curled, in his dark bedroom, his wrinkled face and exhausted body made visible by the brightness of a TV.

My adult eyes registered the effects of the sickness: the weight loss, the weakened posture, the tired eyes. In all my life, I'd never seen him look so feeble. This was, after all, a man who used to lift a heavy ax and split firewood with a single swooping arm.

I'd never seen Pawpaw Jim look so small. And yet, to the child who dwells in my heart, he's still a giant.

He's the giant who gave me my first pocketknife, always keeping his own within a hand's reach in case something needed a trim or cut free. Naturally, his blade dwarfed mine in size and sharpness, like a machete compared to a butter knife.

The giant and his sweet little wife, Mawmaw Sue, got me my first fishing pole as well, a baby blue Mickey Mouse rod that well-equipped my desire to make trophy catches. Armed with powerful muscles, Pawpaw Jim was always near to help me reel in gargantuan fish.

Of course, when you're very young, even the smallest bream can be deemed a whale.

Pawpaw Jim's also the giant whose enormous boots often crushed all sorts of prickly briars to make walking paths for me as we wandered the countryside, his deep, reassuring voice ushering me forward, "Go ahead, Bop." Similarly, with his massive hands, he routinely held openings through barb wire for me, beckoning, "Come on through, Hotdog."

Those hands used to hold plenty of L&M cigarettes, too.

I recall one memorable cigarette incident that happened when Pawpaw Jim took me, my mother and little sister to Disney World, back when I was in early elementary school. To keep us from wandering astray, my mother tied leashes on my and my sister's wrists, and Pawpaw Jim was handed mine.

At first, I enjoyed walking alongside the giant. However, it became increasingly clear that Pawpaw Jim's periodic smoke breaks posed a threat to my fun. At some point, as my sister and non-smoking mother began to head over to wait for admission to a ride, Pawpaw Jim stayed back and lit a cigarette. He planned to catch up with my mother in line once he finished it.

I didn't get this memo.

"You ain't smokin' that cigarette and holdin' my leash!" I barked, snatching my leash and rushing over to my mother. "Here, Mommy."

Hearing my protest, Pawpaw Jim unleashed a rumbling laugh. Of course, his hearing isn't too great these days, but he's always prided himself in having an ear for good gospel music.

If Pawpaw Jim owned a radio station, a variety of old-school gospel songs (e.g., "I Saw the Light") would play throughout each day, beginning and ending with "Amazing Grace."

Gifted with his own musical talent, Pawpaw Jim has always been recognized in our family for his ability to play practically any instrument by ear, his favorites being the harmonica, piano and accordion.

His love for the latter instrument, however, was an acquired taste.

When Pawpaw Jim was a kid, his dad strongly—forcefully—insisted he practice playing the accordion. Streams of tears flowing down his cheeks, a young Pawpaw Jim performed for his dad, who loved the music because it lulled him to sleep.

Of course, what once drew sobs now inspires laughter when Pawpaw Jim reflects on these memories.

That's a good thing, as he has a tremendous smile, even when he lacks his partial denture and resembles a jolly jack-o'-lantern. Furthermore, this very smile, paired with the calmest blue eyes, mirror the tender goodness of his soul.

Pawpaw Jim has spent a lifetime helping people, even during difficult times when he's chosen to be the bigger man, dropping petty pride to embrace higher virtues. Prior to getting sick, he also derived great joy from preaching sermons at church, and sharing the gospel during nursing home visits.

Granted, the sickness has managed to shrink his physique.

But his gentle character, and the warm memories he shares with our family, remain gigantic.

He's still a giant.

Opelika-Auburn News
NOVEMBER 8, 2020

A much younger Pawpaw Jim Sanders is shown holding his daughters, Stacey and Leisa (my aunt and my mother), during the 1970s. Pawpaw Jim passed away on December 8, 2020. This column was read during a eulogy at his funeral on December 11.

SYMPATHETIC PREGNANCY: A CASE OF MOTHER AND SON

The news came months ago, delivered via scribblings on a Starbucks coffee cup. Smiling excitedly—secretively—Kim handed me the drink. She'd asked if I'd meet her inside Target in Tiger Town after work. She wanted me to get a good look at something.

That "something" was a surprising, and well-welcomed, message: I was going to be a daddy again. Months later, an ultrasound revealed that I was going to be a daddy to a son—again!

Naturally, our family is thrilled, especially Kaleb. He's super excited to be getting a little brother. It'll give him a smaller human, a blood-kin minion, to boss around. In fact, Kaleb is so enthused about the whole thing that something fascinating has been going on in our household. I'm assuming you've heard of Couvade syndrome, a.k.a. "sympathetic pregnancy"? It's when men experience similar pregnancy symptoms as their child-bearing mate.

I reckon I went through a little of this when Kim was pregnant with Kaleb, particularly in sharing her difficulty with getting enough sleep and the inevitable weight gain. Of course, the increase in weight was expected of Kim. I, on the other hand, should have set healthier boundaries with calories.

But this time, things have taken a drastic turn. This time it's Kaleb who's being sympathetically pregnant with Kim. And it's certainly a situation that's giving plenty of amusement to help pass the time as we all await the arrival of Kason Michael Huffman.

This all started shortly after we explained to Kaleb that his baby brother is in mommy's tummy. Not to be outdone, Kaleb has since claimed that there's a baby in his tummy too. But not just one, mind you. Initially, there were two babies and then three. Now, he says there are five, and they all kick around so much in his bouncing tummy that I swear those munchkins must be playing leapfrog—that or Kaleb's got a belly full of hyper kangaroos.

It appears my wife may have one of those too. Or at least that's my assumption each time I feel little Kason's movements. Intrigued by these moments as well, Kaleb is prone to grabbing our hands and then quickly placing them on his tummy, the little tummy he sticks out as far as he can. It's hard to believe that five babies can fit in there. Maybe he's having puppies. At this point, it's certainly within the realm of possibility.

Either way, Kaleb and Kim's food cravings are worth noting as well. Lately, Kim has been obsessed with sushi. In fact, a mere utterance of the word sends an electrifying surge of joy through her, instantly lighting up her face and eyes like yard decorations at Christmastime, her mind set on devouring sea creatures wrapped in rice and dried seaweed. Kaleb, meanwhile, has been obsessed with his own special sushi: cheese Goldfish crackers, minus any soy sauce or wasabi.

And then there's the agonizing heartburn, bearing a heat so intense that I'm often torn between fetching Kim some Prilosec or a fire extinguisher. Mimicking his mommy, Kaleb is prone to clutching his chest, whimpering with the utmost dramatic sincerity, "Oh, it burns! It burns!"

There's the nausea, the cramps, and the headaches as well. Plus their inability to get up off the couch without rocking back and forth like turtles. And the mood swings ... perhaps Kaleb says it best, usually after I tease him in ill attempts to win a smile: "You're killing me, Daddy. You're killing me."

As I said, the whole thing has been very entertaining, so much so that I'm not at all aware if I've been sharing any sympathy symptoms with Kim. I reckon Kaleb has shared plenty to cover the both of us many times over.

But there is one thing I know the three of us definitely share: our excitement and high anticipation for welcoming our family's fourth recruit. The joyful looks on our faces summed it up as we observed little Kason's face during the 4D ultrasound.

Kaleb beamed as he looked at the image on the screen, and then, slowly, he put his hand on his tummy.

Opelika-Auburn News
OCTOBER 13, 2019

OH, BROTHER!

Hinted, pleaded, insisted—this is what five-year-old Kaleb did for nine months, nine long months. And then, at long last, on November 24 at precisely 1 p.m., his hints, pleas, and insistence paid off. Kaleb's brother, Kason Michael Huffman, finally decided to "pop out" of his mommy's tummy. Now we just can't stop smiling each time we gaze upon our baby's sweet face.

Naturally, Kaleb is absolutely elated that he's now officially a "big brother." I imagine pretty soon he'll be inquiring about whether he can take advantage of any big brother discounts at restaurants and movie theaters. It all comes with the territory, or should.

In fact, Kaleb may have already sent a letter to Congress, advocating for the honorary implementation of "Big Brother Day." Not to be confused with the observation of National Brothers Day on May 24, Big Brother Day will mark a momentous celebration when everyone—namely younger siblings—will praise their big and more seasoned brothers.

As a big brother myself, I fully endorse this proposal. After all, it's only fair that we big bros gain the acknowledgement we so righteously deserve for our many sacrifices: loss of full parental attention; taking turns with practically everything; sharing toys we forgot we had but suddenly can't live without, etc. This is not to mention all the times we're held accountable and prompted to "set a good example" for the naïve little tykes.

I reckon big sisters make these same sacrifices too, and we could certainly use their help to strengthen our numbers and further our cause for well-deserved glorification. Therefore, it makes perfect sense to include them in the proposal's final draft: Big Brother (and by necessity, Big Sister) Day. Just imagine that exact title on a big, shiny banner.

Yessiree, a national holiday would help us at least gain some restitution—I mean, recognition—for our humble roles in life. Otherwise, we'll simply have to resort to other tactics for settling scores between older and younger siblings.

Take Pawpaw Jim and his younger brother, Uncle Louis, who've waged a cosmic bet between one another, a no-holds-barred showdown that's expected to embolden the "Absolute Best" between them and ultimately cap their sibling rivalry: whoever has the most toys when they die, wins. Lord, please have mercy on us if they tie.

Of course, some sibling rivalries are a bit more complex, like the one that was between my father and his late brother, "Son," a cross-eyed and very ornery Siamese cat who Pawpaw Buck adopted as a kitten from a friend. And, folks, Pawpaw Buck adored his furry son, often warning his human son, "Now, Doe Doe, don't be mean to your brother."

That cat could do no wrong. Nope, not even when Son threw tantrums and tore their country home slap up, even knotting together necklaces, when he didn't get to ride downtown in Buck's car. Nor the times when my teenage father would come home late on the weekends, easing his way to the living room couch to keep from waking his daddy, and afterward awaken in terror to something sitting on his chest.

A pair of blueish-gray eyes would be staring down intently into his.

My father says Son did have some pretty eyes, like sparkling crystals. But they sure looked pretty dang evil when illuminated by the brightness from the old light pole outside that shone through the living room window by the couch.

"Don't be mean to your brother"—easier said than done, especially when you feel cheated, as in my case. I'm referring to the day I was introduced to my little sister, Hannah.

It is nothing against her, per se. It's just that I'd already picked the baby we were supposed to have taken home prior to Hannah's debut.

This all happened sometime shortly after my mother started going into labor and my great-grandfather had taken a nearly four-year-old me to go look at the newborns in the hospital nursery. Staring through the glass, I spotted the perfect sibling: a precious baby with curly black hair and a complexion infinitely darker than mine.

"I want that one right there," I said, confident in the superbness of my selection. Eager to get my order in, I wasted no time telling my mother that she could get out of bed and come on home. I'd picked the baby.

At least I thought I did. Somehow my order had gotten mixed up, or someone deliberately sabotaged it. Because the baby I was introduced to was definitely not the one I'd carefully handpicked. This one shared my exact complexion. And she was bald.

That's life, I reckon. My son Kaleb, on the other hand, is very content with the baby we brought home, constantly kissing and telling Kason, "Yay! I'm so happy you finally popped out! I love you!"

Still, I've begun to sense a hint of turbulence between them. It was sparked just the other day, when we were all downstairs at home. Kaleb was busy playing a game, and Kason started crying for a bottle.

As I headed over to get Kason, Kim got up to make her final trip upstairs for the day. But before she got past the couch, she received a sincere request from Kaleb, who was having some difficulty tuning out his little brother: "Mommy, can you take the baby upstairs so he don't bother me?"

And here's where it all starts ... but at least it's what Kaleb hinted, pleaded, and insisted he wanted.

Opelika-Auburn News
DECEMBER 8, 2019

WATCH 'EM GROW

A little chimpanzee sits on my desk.

Approximately two inches in height, the plastic chimp watches me each day, ears super alert, its left hand forever scratching the back of its head in a perpetual state of confusion. It's the same gesture I make when I'm routinely absorbed in the special world that's always under construction by my five-year-old son Kaleb, who gave me the chimp as a Christmas gift.

Kaleb sees things that I can't—at least not at first anyway—like bubbling rivers of lava, pretend roads filled with honking traffic, varieties of spooky ghosts and scary monsters, and seas of massive sharks bearing endless rows of razor-sharp chompers. We may encounter these and many more phenomena on a given day, at given times, during the random adventures and games Kaleb creates for us to play. In fact, the rules to these adventures and games can change on a whim, and Kaleb expects you to realize these changes the exact moment he himself becomes aware of them.

"Daddy! The button to stop the dinosaurs from gettin' us isn't over there anymore! It's over *here* now! You gotta hurry!"

Yet again, I'm left scratchin' my noggin.

Of course, this is all very amusing to Kaleb's baby brother, Kason, who smiles and coos while watching his big brother's antics. Their brotherhood has blasted off to a great start, and while I certainly can't see into the future, I hope their bond only keeps getting stronger, like the bond shared between two of my kin folk when they were young boys. Wandering the countryside many decades ago, these boys loved to hunt and skin rabbits, usually selling their kills to the old lady who lived nearby.

One day they desperately wanted to earn some money, but no rabbits could be found hopping around. Hell-bent on getting some cash, this resourceful duo went on the hunt for something—anything—else. They came across a cat.

"That ain't no rabbit!" the old lady barked as they made their offer. Persisting, the boys combined their persuasive skills to help keep the prospective business deal afloat.

"It is *too* a rabbit!"

"That's a sho'nuff for-real rabbit, ma'am! Skinned it ourselves."

Eventually, the old lady did buy it, but she never wavered from her conviction: "That ain't no rabbit." Teamwork, folks.

I hope my sons make a good team. I also hope they don't constantly trade fists every time they disagree, like my great-great-uncles, Leon and Bill Sutton, did when they were youngsters in the 1930s. Uncle Leon was set in his ways at a very young age, absolutely refusing to accept anything—fact, observation, suggestion—that remotely clashed with any beliefs he stored up in his head. Uncle Bill, on the other hand, was infinitely more open-minded and very prone to debate and challenge his older brother.

His nose sure suffered for it.

The two argued over everything, including planetology. A staunch flat-Earther, Uncle Leon's blood always boiled when Uncle Bill stood his ground and referenced the globe he saw at the schoolhouse.

Now, both Leon and Bill spent the majority—if not all—of their youths working on their family's farm. But Bill got a bit more schooling than Leon did. Still, Uncle Leon didn't care what some stinkin' schoolhouse globe said.

"Of course the Earth is flat! Look here, the ground you walk on is flat. If the damn thing were round, you'd keep falling over. Any idiot knows you can't walk on something shaped like a wheel, unless you're some sort of circus clown."

But Uncle Bill disagreed, and that's when words turned to fists. Uncle Leon whooped Uncle Bill so bad once that their sister, Reoma, rushed over to help Bill up off the ground, whispering to him, "Bill, just go on and agree with him, so he won't beat you up. You don't have to really agree with him. Just pretend like you do, so he won't bust your nose no more."

But Uncle Bill refused. "He's *wrong*, and I'm gonna keep *tellin'* him he's wrong."

I reckon brothers are gonna fight in some way or another. But hopefully Kaleb won't pull no stunts with Kason like Pawpaw Buck Huffman did with his little sister, Betty Jean, like the time an eight-year-old Buck buried a three-year-old Betty Jean in the woodpile. Their mother had come in from planting sweet potatoes and couldn't find her baby girl. Finally, she asked Buck if he'd seen her.

"Oh yeah, I buried her in the woodpile out back," he said. And that's where Aunt Betty Jean was, sound asleep under a pile of mostly sticks, wood chips, and splinters.

Another time, Buck set Aunt Betty Jean in his sights with his BB gun. Only she ducked in time, and the BB hit the dresser mirror behind her, damaging one of the nicest pieces of furniture their family had.

There also was the time a young Buck managed to accidentally hit Aunt Betty Jean with his motorcycle, while she was walking down the road. Luckily, he'd just turned onto the road and wasn't going too fast. But he knocked his sister to the ground, where she laid until Buck turned around about a mile up the road and came back to check on her. "Well, Betty Jean, I didn't mean to kill ya," he said.

Fortunately, she wasn't hurt, just surprised.

With any luck, my boys will keep these kinds of surprises at a minimum. More than anything, though, I hope they band together and support one another when times get tough, just like all my grandparents and great-grandparents did (and do) with their siblings.

True, some of them may have bickered like the dickens, threatening to unleash all sorts of hell on each other when tempers flared, but they all were the first to show up when one or the other needed help—guaranteed.

In the meantime, I'm enjoying watching my boys grow. I'm watching with the same intense excitement that illuminates my Kaleb's face when he finds a brand new rock for the little plastic container he calls his "treasure chest" or when he checks on the little vegetables he helped his mommy plant.

"Daddy, listen! I think I hear them growing!"

Kason seems to share his big brother's enthusiasm. He's all smiles too.

I'm smiling and listening as well, watching my boys grow … and scratchin' the back of my head the whole time.

Opelika-Auburn News
APRIL 12, 2020

ACKNOWLEDGMENTS

Sincerest thanks goes to my first editor and good buddy, Doug Sanders Jr., for all the encouragement he's given me over the years. He is, hands down, one of the biggest blessings in my life. Another massive heap of gratitude goes to Tonya Balaam-Reed, copy and features editor of the *Opelika-Auburn News*. She is, to use her own word, "cooltastic." I also want to thank all the other editors at media outlets who've offered valuable feedback and published my work. Finally, I want to express my appreciation to all the folks who've devoted time, and perhaps a good cup of coffee or two, reading the stuff under my byline. This, naturally, includes my wife, Kim, who, along with our sons Kaleb and Kason, keeps inspiring me to put my voice on paper.

ABOUT THE AUTHOR

Keith Huffman is a licensed professional counselor who helps his clients cope with and overcome psychological hardships. A graduate of the University of Alabama, he also has worked as a journalist, writing for the *Pickens County Herald* and *Opelika-Auburn News*, where he contributes a feature column. He lives in Alabama with his family.